FAITH FORMATION in VITAL Congregations

FAITH ▲
FORMATION
◀ in VITAL ▶
Congregations
∨

Marian R. Plant

Anthony B. Robinson, Series Editor

THE
PILGRIM
PRESS
Cleveland

Dedication

To David, my loving spousal unit:

Here's the book you said I had to write.

And to Virginia Less, my "Elizabeth."

The Pilgrim Press, 700 Prospect Avenue East, Cleveland, Ohio 44115
thepilgrimpress.com

© 2009 Marian R. Plant

Scripture quotations are from the *New Revised Standard Version of the Bible*,
©1989 by the Division of Christian Education of the National Council of
the Churches of Christ in the United States of America and are used by
permission. Changes have been made for inclusivity.

Printed in the United States of America on acid-free paper.

14 13 12 11 10 09   5 4 3 2

Library of Congress Cataloging-in-Publication Data

Plant, Marian R., 1951—

   Faith formation in vital congregations / Marian R. Plant.

   p. cm. — (Congregational vitality series)

   ISBN 13: 978-0-8298-1813-0 (alk. paper)

   1. Chrstian education of adults. I. Title.

BV1488.P58 2009

 268'.434—dc22

                                    2007045690

Contents

Foreword

Whether you use the words "Christian Education," "Christian Formation," "Sunday School," "Adult Education," or "the Teaching Ministry of the Church," if you are concerned about how people grow in the Christian faith, this book is for you. While each of these terms has a somewhat different emphasis, all of them point to a critical area of the church's life and ministry: how do congregations in today's world teach, form and sustain believers? This crucial topic is the one Marian Plant takes on in this important contribution to our series of resources for vital congregations.

Why are Christian education and formation such important topics today? The short answer is the one Dorothy famously remarked to her faithful dog Toto in the classic movie, "The Wizard of Oz." "Toto," said Dorothy after they had been dropped by the twister, "I've got a feeling we're not in Kansas anymore."

We used to live in "Kansas," that is, the world of North American Christendom. In that world, society and church were woven together in many mutually supportive ways. It was easier, in many respects, to do Christian education and formation than it is today. For one thing, we didn't face the competition of youth sports and a myriad of other activities on Sundays. For another, public schools were partners to the church. My elementary school day, fifty years ago, began with the Pledge of Allegiance, a reading from the Bible and a prayer. The church had a good deal of support from the culture.

By and large, that's over. We no longer live in that world and we can no longer depend on the culture to do Christian formation for us. North American society today is officially secular, religiously pluralistic, and racially and ethnically diverse. And that is a big change in the North American landscape.

Since we can no longer depend on the culture to do Christian formation for us, we have the opportunity to figure out how to do it ourselves. And this is, however challenging at times, a genuine and exciting opportunity. All over North America, churches are discovering new ways to do both education and spiritual formation with adults, youth and children.

Marian Plant's book will be a terrific guide for congregations, Christian education boards, church educators and pastoral leaders who seek to rise to these new challenges and to the opportunity of doing faithful and fruitful Christian education and formation today.

You'll find that Marian thinks and writes with both wit and enthusiasm. Moreover, she practices what she preaches. She does not just talk "at" you. She engages you. She helps you do your own work as you take on questions about how we learn and how we teach in this new time.

Marian writes as a gifted educator and teacher of the church, as a parent, and as a person of faith. Her broad knowledge, wide experience, and solid grounding in this work make this book pertinent, accessible and enormously helpful for congregations in our new time.

Anthony B. Robinson
Editor, Congregational Vitality Series

Introduction

> You like potato and I like potahto,
> You like tomato and I like tomahto.
> Potato, potahto,
> Tomato, tomahto,
> Let's call the whole thing off,
> Let's call the whole thing off.

Curious way to begin a book on adult Christian formation for vital congregations, isn't it? A good metaphor though for the local church's approach to the subject. Terms alone, for instance, can cause us to throw up our hands in exasperation or dismay.

> You like education and I like formation,
> You like un-churched and I like pre-churched.
> Education, formation,
> Un-churched, pre-churched,
> Let's call the whole thing off,
> Let's call the whole thing off.

Since you've picked up this book and have at least read this far, it's safe to assume you are far from willing to "call the whole thing off" even if you do find yourself throwing up your hands from time to time.

When Anthony Robinson, general editor of the *Vital Congregations* series, and I were first in communication about the focus of this book he wrote:

> I believe that we want a major focus of this book to be adult Christian formation, or how adults who have either been in the church a long time, never been in the church, or are returning with little background are then formed in faith and discipleship.

This is the task I have joyfully undertaken. There is much to be done in the area of adult Christian formation. Fortunately much attention from a variety of quarters is contributing to an expanding understanding of the adults we hope to reach and engage in Christian formation, and a growing bank of resources from which to draw. The good work done by Dorothy Bass and her colleagues in the Valparaiso Project on practices of faith is reawakening an interest in and appreciation for the relevance of ancient practices for Christian living and spiritual wholeness in our lives of faith and faithfulness in the complex, often overwhelming, anxious 21st century. Equally important is the work of numerous authors and practitioners such as Richard Foster, Kathleen Norris, Jill Kimberly Hartwell Geoffrion (labyrinth), Barbara A. Sheehan (spiritual companionship), Brett Webb-Mitchell (pilgrimage) and others in resurrecting foundational Christian spiritual disciplines and spirituality, much of which dropped by the wayside as churches and denominations were challenged by seismic shifts in culture first by the Industrial Revolution, then the technology explosion, and all the ramifications of the modern and post-modern ages. Page through denominational book and resource catalogues or go to the online websites and you will find fine materials to assist individuals and church leaders in understanding and adopting these disciplines into their lives.

In a different vain but no less important is the work of Bill Easum and Tom Bandy, Walt Kallestad, George Bullard, Paul Borden and Luther Snow on church revitalization and the transforming of local churches to missioning and disciple-ing communities of faith. Also from still another vain comes ongoing work with Howard Gardner's theory of multiple intelligences and the adult learner that continues to enrich our understanding of the role intelligences such as kinesthetic, musical, interpersonal and intrapersonal have in connecting people with the living heritage of the Christian faith, fruitful discipleship, and engagement with the biblical texts. We are coming to realize that the cognitive (i.e. the verbal + written + logical) such as we see in traditional sermons, lecture-style teaching, and start-here-and-go-to-there approaches, are not enough to provide satisfying Christian formation experiences. Tapping the full collection of multiple intelligences enhances individuals' ability to engage in and deepen their Christian life of faith and discipleship.

So the good news (always lead with the good news, right?) is that lots of work has gone on and continues to go one on behalf of people seeking faith and faithful responses in their lives within the world, and on behalf of those charged with the responsibility of crafting and implementing processes and programs that further Christian formation across the various populations and participants crossing the thresholds of our churches.

The not-so-good news is that you — ordained or lay pastor, professional church educator, family life coordinator, educational ministry volunteer, member of a committee, task force, or board — cannot simply pick up this or that resource, this or that packaged program, this or that workshop or seminar and "solve" Christian formation. You are going to have to do some ground work, some foundation construction, even some excavation. You are going to have to build, in essence, a roadbed before you invest in vehicles (i.e. resources, programs, ministries). Remember Isaiah's declaration as echoed by John the Baptist:

> "Prepare the way of the Lord, make his path straight. Every valley shall be filled, and every mountain and hill shall be made low, and the crooked shall be made straight, and the rough ways made smooth...."
>
> (Luke 4b–5 NRSV)

You've got to get the graders and the pavers out. First the roadbed, then the pavement, then the travel!

That's where this book comes in. Its job — my job — is to provide frameworks for doing the necessary roadbed work and provide strategies for not only building the road(s), but also for traveling forward in adult Christian formation. Within these pages you will find

- Think Pieces that are short essays on particularly critical issues
- Point in Time exercises designed to engage you in processes that put your experience and contextual setting into dialogue with the current theories and practices described above
- strategies for developing ministries that spark, ignite, and sustain adult Christian formation
- examples to help illustrate the strategies
- stories from the lives and ministries of friends, colleagues, and parishioners that put a human face on all this.

It has been my true pleasure to write this book for you. I invite you to mine it for the gems you can use. I encourage you to "do the hard work" rather than look for shortcuts. Your ministry — Christ's ministry — and the vitality of the congregation you serve are too important for quick fixes that simply are that... quick fixes with no faith formative and transformative sustainability. Along the way enjoy the journey and the fruits it will bring.

This book is mine, but I could not write it alone. Innumerable (as in many, many, MANY) thanks belong to the trusting planning committees of the Minnesota Conference of the United Church of Christ Educators, the Myrtle

Beach Seminar by the Sea Annual Continuing Education Event for Clergy and Laity, the Indiana-Kentucky Conference of the United Church of Christ Clergy Education Day, and the Great Lakes Association of United Church Educators who invited me into their day-long, weekend-long, and week-long events as leader/presenter/facilitator, for out of those fertile fields of preparation and engagement much of what is in this book has sprouted and matured. Thanks also belong to the United Church of Christ Partners in Education, especially "Kenny O and the Miracle-ettes" plus Debbie Gline Allen, for their encouragement and uncanny, though not unexpected, insights, wisdom, and irreplaceable humor over the years. Then there is Patricia Goldberg, who pointed down the length of a conference table at me while saying "We know who could write this book," and two of my Defiance College colleagues: MC Harper, my mentor and friend who companioned me through the entire creative and fine-tuning process, and Amy Drees, who tackled several graphic design challenges from my end for the website component of this project.

On the Pilgrim Press side of the house, thanks belong to David Shoen, for leaking my name to Anthony (Tony) Robinson, the Vital Congregations series editor, and to Tony for following up on that leak, to my Pilgrim Press editor Kim Sadler (to whom I owe at least 119 "late coupons"), and to my copyeditor extraordinaire Katherine Larson (who never saw this paragraph — I wanted to surprise her – and therefore is not responsible for mistakes of grammar, punctuation, or syntax herein).

No one evolves into who they are in a vacuum, or who they will yet become. And while writing by committee would be patently ugly, writing surrounded by so great a cloud of witnesses and amidst the communion of saints is a wonderment!

One

Jesus Welcomed Children and Taught Adults: Reality Check for Local Churches

"Jesus welcomed children and taught adults. We welcome adults and teach children. Someone's got this backwards, and I don't think it was Jesus."[1]

In this chapter we're going to tackle four issues that are basic to creating and sustaining environments of fruitful Christian formation. To use a current vernacular, we might talk about this in terms of Christian formation sustainability. Congregations and leaders will be well on their way to creating or enhancing Christian formation sustainability once they do a reality check to identify how their assumptions and ministries align with these basics.

✓ Jesus welcomed children and taught adults
✓ Christian education ≠ Sunday school for kids
✓ Christian formation is empowered/powered by Christian education
✓ Christian formation is process, not product

Jesus Welcomed Children and Taught Adults

• Read Mark 10:13–16

When Jesus gathered the children into his arms, he *blessed them*. There was no children's sermon, no flannel board, no object lesson, no take-home papers. He *welcomed* them and he *blessed* them. Jesus aimed the message of that teachable moment at the adults clustered around him. On a different occasion Jesus used a child to drive home a point to his disciples.

• Read Matthew 18:1–6

The scriptural narratives recount numerous sessions — impromptu as well as planned — during which Jesus engages the adults around issues of social justice, prayer, care for neighbor, authentic faith practices, healing and wholeness, and the realm of God in their midst and in their future. Take a moment and refresh your memory with these scriptural narratives. Notice the wonderful variations in context, audiences, and individuals Jesus taught.

• Matthew 4:23
• Matthew 5:1–3
• Matthew 13:34, 36
• Mark 5:1–3
• Luke 10:25–37
• Luke 11:1–4
• Luke 12:13–16
• Luke 14: 1–6
• John 8:2–11

Individuals, small groups, "crowds", antagonists, commoners, disciples… all were adults. There's no way around it. Jesus set the model for Christian formation's primary methodology — teaching and learning — and the original constituency was adults.

Christian Education ≠ Sunday School for Kids

Jesus' focus on adults provides a reality check for the church and clergy's tendency to relate teaching and learning rightly with Christian education, but then erroneously to equate Christian education primarily with children and

Sunday school and put all their formation "eggs" in a single basket: formation = Sunday school + children. A similarly prevalent "eggs in a basket" model is the formation = confirmation + youth model.

Point-in-Time Exercise: How Many Eggs Are in Your Adult Faith Formation Basket?

■ Using a copy of the current church budget, compute the percentages for each category below.

_____% goes to formation/education of children and youth, not counting Sunday morning
_____% goes to adult formation/education, not counting Sunday morning
_____% goes to formation/education of adults on Sunday morning
_____% goes to formation/education of children and youth on Sunday morning

■ Using the approximate number of hours worked each week, compute the percentages for each category below.

_____% of the pastor(s) time each week goes into formation/education of children and youth. List what you count, e.g., children's sermon, confirmation
_____% of the pastor(s) time each week goes into formation/education of adults. List what you count, e.g., mid-week Bible study, sermon preparation and delivery

■ Using active volunteer numbers of the church, compute the percentages for each category below. To figure the percent you will need to estimate the total number of volunteers involved in all aspects of the church's ministry and mission, including regular and special events.

_____% of volunteers active in leadership of formation/education of children and youth. List what you count, e.g., church school teachers, children's choir director
_____% of volunteers active in leadership of formation/education of adults. List what you count, e.g., youth group leaders, church school teachers

■ Now sketch three pie charts: (1) illustrating the budget percentages, (2) illustrating the pastoral time percentages, and (3) illustrating the volunteer percentages.

Lay the charts side by side. What do you notice? Is there at least equal attention, time, financial support, and staffing — volunteer or paid — designated for Christian faith formation of adults as for children and youth? If so, what else might be envisioned to build upon what is already in place, so that adults' faith and discipleship does not plateau or stagnate? On the other hand, do the percentages suggest unequal amounts of attention, time, financial support, and staffing — volunteer or paid — designated for the various age groups, with adult faith formation/education on the lesser side? If so, the challenge is three-fold: to envision adult Christian formation with a wider lens, to explore possibilities for engaging in meaningful ministries that support and foster Christian faith formation and discipleship in adults, and to pilot some of those ministries, whether totally new or simply reshaped. Help in moving forward is offered throughout this book.

Part of the reason local churches and clergy become locked into narrow models of formation such as formation = Sunday school + children and formation = confirmation + youth is that, over the years, these became the familiar models explicitly identified as Christian education and faith formation. Think of it like this: If the only things you'd ever had pointed out to you as "automobiles" were Fords and Dodges, you'd likely ignore things called Buicks, Chryslers, and VWs when you were shopping for a car. What I want laity and clergy alike to recognize is that what most of them have been calling Christian education is just one small town's auto showroom with the most basic four-cylinder models. Understanding and undertaking the process of Christian formation with the prospect of only these basic models would be unimaginable at worst, formidable at best.

Fortunately, Christian education brings incredible strengths to the challenge. The five listed below provide the big picture for understanding the depth and breadth of Christian education. Out of this depth and breadth, out of this theoretical and theological paradigm, all the forms and programs, ideas and concrete resources that we need can be developed. If we stay with the quirky automobile analogy, think of the strengths as the auto industry's research and development, design, engineering, and mechanic specialists out of which will flow the combined fleets of all the auto companies put together.

1. Christian education is about:

- understanding human beings in all their made-in-God's-image complexities
- meeting child, youth, and adult where and when they are
- inviting them into the sacred and saving journey
- and making a road of faith with them by walking it together.

2. Christian education has the capacity to inform, influence, enhance, confirm, challenge, redirect, critique, and energize every other aspect of ministry when one is equipped and grounded in it. Conversely, Christian education practice has the potential to be informed, influenced, enhanced, confirmed, challenged, redirected, critiqued, and energized by all other aspects of ministry when one understands Christian education as more than successful administration of church school programs and youth groups.

3. Christian education embodies, celebrates, and employs a unique union of rich, explicitly Christian disciplines and scholarship . . .

- biblical and theological studies; worship and sacraments; preaching; evangelism; church history, doctrine, and tradition; spirituality, prayer and meditation; pastoral care; mission and service; catechesis and *didache* . . .

. . . with insightful social science disciplines and scholarship . . .

- psychology, particularly developmental psychology; educational theory and methods; sociology; multicultural studies, gender studies, qualitative and quantitative research, and so forth.

4. Christian education recognizes the profound importance of story and fashions frameworks for hearing, telling, valuing and confirming story:

- individual life story
- faith-journey story
- the biblical story and stories
- the church's story

The profound importance of story cannot be overestimated. The profound transformative power in telling and hearing story must not be underestimated.

5. Christian education, by its very nature, provides the wherewithal to affect individuals of any and all ages — cradle to grave. Christian education is also essential for any and all ages.

- What we learn and experience of God, Christ, the Holy Spirit, what we learn and experience of unconditional love, forgiveness, repentance and divine guidance as children (or what we do not learn and experience as children) impacts who and what we are as adults.
- What we learn and experience of God, Christ, the Holy Spirit, what we learn and experience of unconditional love, forgiveness, repentance and divine guidance as adults (or what we don't learn and experience as adults), impacts how we make sense of our childhood and youth, and how we make meaning and purpose of our adult lives.

Christian Formation is Empowered/Powered by Christian Education

Like Siamese twins, Christian education and Christian formation are inseparable and, at their best, nearly indistinguishable. To assume one can "do" Christian formation without benefit of Christian education is counterproductive or is, as my older son would say, "just wrong!"

Wrong also is the belief, assumption, or pipedream that there is (or can be) such a thing as any one workshop, any one study series, or any one model to form adults' faith. Faith and its companion discipleship do not come about through, for instance, a "banking" model, i.e., the leader "deposits" information into an individual and the individual "gains" faith and then "does" discipleship.[2] Formation of Christian adults is process — process that equips and nurtures in the here-and-now, plus process that will reequip and re-nurture throughout the adult Christian's life.

This is a far cry from the formation = Sunday school + children model dominating so many congregations' landscapes and so many clergy's perspectives. This is a far cry from the formation = confirmation + youth model that is just as prevalent.

Adults are meaning-makers. Adults raise questions of faith out of the lives they have lived in earlier years. *What did that mean? Why did that happen? Am I responsible for _____? Is there a way to mend that which is broken? Can God love me after what I've done? I've made my own way. What's God got to do with it?*

> Hank: It just hit me: God is good. We have heard that forever. Creation is of God so creation must be good. I am a product of creation. I am created out of creation and I must be good even though I can do evil things. I am accepted. It just flipped it open. Acceptance. We can be guilty of all kinds of things but I don't have to live with that as the front thought. A thought that I have got to do something to overcome the guilt. It was that flash that I realized was very significant. Probably *the* significant turning point for me in how I live my life.[3]

Adults raise questions of faith out of the lives they live right now. *How can I be patriotic and follow the Prince of Peace? I've worked hard for my modest financial security. I've earned my comforts. Why do I have to simplify my life to save creation from environmental catastrophe? We were just discovering each other again — falling in love all over again. Why cancer now? Why cancer at all?*

> Sam: I came to understand that for me to sit on the whatever committee and meet faithfully with them every Wednesday night from 7 to 9, or once a month on Wednesday night from 7 to 9, and argue about the parking lot, is unfaithful to who I am — while there are people who, as it's played out in my life, need housing. This is only about me. This is only about me. . . . But for me, that would be just really a bankruptcy of values to be sitting there on Wednesday night as a conscious choice to not be sitting across the table at Denny's [Restaurant] from a person who's really in need. And trying to figure out what resources are available — and how many fish [as in the loaves and fishes miracle] can I bring to the table here tonight.[4]

Throughout the life of Christianity, the church as institution and living body of Christ has sought to meet the human quest for meaning-making. Most often the church did this through articulating the salvation narrative of the life, death, and resurrection of Jesus who is the Christ, the redeemer and savior of the world. Beginning in simple yet profound declarations of belief evidenced in the earliest baptismal confessions, the salvation narrative evolved into creedal formulas as more complex issues compelled the church to provide clarifications on once-presumed-obvious theology. Over time, the creedal formulas birthed catechisms for instruction of those born into the households of faith and those converted to Christianity. Each embodiment of the salvation narrative served as framework for meaning-making and, while we may cringe at some of the timbers in the various frameworks, the reality remains: fundamental questions raised by adults of every generation were given answer by the church.

Students of church history will be quick to point out how narrow-minded and self-serving various leaders and cadres of leaders within the church have been throughout the centuries. The preoccupations with power and self-aggrandizement handicapped the common parishioners' faith formation by skewing the church's interpretation of the salvation narrative and, therefore, each Christian's requirements of discipleship. Nonetheless, people still had a theological framework, albeit warped around some edges, for making sense of and giving purpose to their lives.

Christian formation has always occurred within specific contexts, always within specific time periods, always with the resources available and, most effectively, when the people's needs within that specific context and time were identified and taken seriously. However, even at the height of Christendom's power and influence in Western Europe, the church's framework for meaning-making wasn't the only one available. Much to the consternation of local church pastors and educators today, the twenty-first century church's framework for meaning-making isn't the only one out there either.

The culture of the larger society in which the twenty-first century church is embedded offers its tantalizing and accessible take on meaning-making. Accessible because we are immersed in it day in and day out from the beginning. Tantalizing because everything offered looks "perfect" and "just for me," and promises to turn me into the "real" me at the press of a button, flick of a switch, or swipe of a credit card. We learn this framework of meaning-making in the market place and in the public school. We are shaped by it in the school hallways, cafeterias, and locker rooms, and by the advertisements we see, hear, and read. We take our cues about our place and role in it from the playground, athletic fields, academic ranking, television, movies, reality shows and video games. We buy into it first with our allowances; next with our baby-sitting, lawn-mowing, and paper routes; then with our cell phones and iPods, text-messaging and instant digital photos; and ultimately with our job choices, wages and salaries, rents, mortgages, and car purchases. We know its colors and shapes and sounds so well that we can pick out any particular decade by the length of skirt, width of pant leg, type of shirt, style of shoe, and "Oh, my gosh, *look at that hair!*" Plus, we want it all, for this is obviously what gives meaning and purpose to life.

To believe that secular society, even twenty-first century North American society, provides authentic frameworks for adult Christian meaning-making is foolishness. To believe that adults in our churches are not swayed by the socio-cultural meaning-making framework is equal foolishness. To believe that there was once upon a time when the culture's lure was powerless on Christians is the greatest foolishness. Jesus' message to his generation thrummed with the call to counter-culture. It thrums with that same counter-cultural call today. That's why it is critical that clergy and congregations turn up the volume on Jesus' counter-cultural call and turn their attention to faith formation and faith re-formation of adults.

One starting point is available to all local congregations: the ability to get a picture of what faith formation models are up-and-running in their setting, and then to ask some evocative questions of those models. Pastors and laity alike become trapped in teaching-learning routines that can unintentionally truncate adult Christian formation. Take, for example, the Sunday morning adult education class that the pastor teaches. This class is frequently built on the confirmation class model with which the pastor is most familiar, or the teacher-student model of the pastor's seminary class days.

- There is content to be "taught." Sometimes the content is from a book selected by the pastor or requested by the class, such as Harold Kushner's *Why Bad Things Happen to Good People* or Marcus Borg's *The Heart of Christianity*. Sometimes the content is from a curricular resource, either denominationally produced, e.g., *The Present Word* or *Seasons of the Spirit* or ecumenically available, e.g., *Living the Questions* or Bill Moyer's *Genesis* video series. Content comes from somewhere.
- There is preparation for the session, at minimum by the pastor who will "teach" the day's lesson. Adult participants may or may not be encouraged to read the lesson or chapter in preparation for each week. The operative word here is "encouraged." Notice it is not "expected" or "required."
- There is presentation of information. The pastor lectures from notes, uses power point, flipcharts, handouts, quotes from the book, and so forth. Or

the pastor may use a question-and-answer format to lead the class through the information.

• There may be discussion, often initiated and directed by the pastor.
• There is an end to the class time. The pastor heads off to lead worship. The adult participants go in their various directions.

In this model, the routine is comfortable for those who attend. But does it promote and further develop the formation of adults as Christian?

Borrowing from assessment principles found in best educational practices,[5] here are questions both pastor and participants need to ask and answer.

1. What is the goal of the Sunday morning adult education class? Alternative: What is the primary goal of the pastor relative to the class? What is the primary goal of the participants?

2. Does the goal of the current topic align with the goal of the class? How or how not?

3. What is/are the desired outcome(s) of engaging in the current topic?

4. Does/do the desired outcome(s) align with the goal of the class?

5. Is/are the outcomes passive or active, or somewhere in between? For example, a passive outcome for the study of Jesus' parables would be for class participants to know about the structure and form of biblical parables. A quasi-active outcome would be for the class participants to suggest ways to live out various parable messages, whereas an active outcome would be for the class to identify and commit to specific changes in their personal, relational, or public actions based on application of a parable's message in today's content. Such an active outcome could even include commitments to report regularly to one another on their personal change, hold each other mutually accountable, and support one another over the next two years.

Notice the significant difference between passive, quasi-active, and active outcomes? Now consider those differences in light of John Dewey's observation that, "The belief that all genuine education comes about through experience does not mean that all experiences are genuinely or equally educative."[6] Our best hope for adults is realized when formation engages discipleship.

There's one more question pastors and participants need to ask and answer:

6. Are the goals and outcomes explicit? In other words, does anyone know what the goals and outcomes are for the Sunday morning adult education class? Does everyone? How do you know? Would the pastor and participants be able to name the goals and outcomes?

If the language and approach described above seem out of place or unusual to you, especially in the context of the church, you are not alone. Few congregational leaders — pastors or laity — bring questions regarding goals and outcomes to the table as educational ministries are proposed and planned. Fewer still ask the questions of educational ministries that already exist and require maintenance.

This is a sad but illuminating condition. Sad, as Jim Wilhoit points out, in that:

> The current crisis in Christian education stems, in large measure, from a lack of clear purpose at the grassroots level. The people most directly involved in Christian education — Sunday-school teachers, youth counselors, and Bible-study leaders — often have no idea of the ultimate purpose of their educational endeavors. The teacher of an adult class may be told that the curriculum for the next quarter is to study the Book of Acts. Yet the reason for selecting Acts — or for studying Isaiah during the current quarter — may be clear to no one. Or consider a children's department where most of the time is spent on crafts and workbooks that have only an incidental relationship to the Bible passage of the week. The teachers believe that they should not bore the children, so they do their best to make the class a lot of fun. Often, however, no one knows the ultimate purpose for the class.[7]

The condition is also illuminating in that, once acknowledged, it offers potential to transform otherwise un-purposed or under-purposed educational ministries to formative ministries of adult Christians. I'll return to this a little later in the chapter. For the moment I invite you to explore several more examples of teaching-learning routines that can unintentionally truncate Christian formation in adults. You'll be using the Point-in-Time Exercise below for this exploration. Then we'll look at some strategies for transforming the routines into more intentional formation opportunities.

Point-in-Time Exercise: What's in Your Teaching-Learning Routine?

■ The following series of questions will look familiar. It is an adaptation of the one used with the Sunday morning adult education class above. Here's how it works.

■ Select at least three educational ministries or programs offered by your local church. Complete the questions for each of those ministries or programs. You can have participants as well as leaders complete the questions. This is best done individually, not as a group process. If a group is lay-led, be sure the pastor(s) also completes the questions for that group.

■ Wondering what falls into the category "teaching-learning routines"? Here are some suggestions just to get you started. Remember, the focus of this Point-in-Time exercise is adult educational ministries and programs.

Sunday Morning Adult Education Class (There may be more than one in your church)
Evening Lenten Study Series
Weekly Bible Study
Thursday Evening Discussion Group
Young Adult Class
Special Topics Series
Women's Bible Study
Men's Bible Study
Parenting Group
Book Discussion Group

Don't get stalled if none of these fit the exact educational ministries and programs of your church. Go with what you have!

■ Now for the questions.

1. What is the *goal* of the educational ministry/program? If there is more than one goal, list them in order of importance, i.e., primary goal, secondary goal, other. Is/are the goal(s) explicit? In other words, does everyone know what they are? Does anyone?
2. What is the goal of the current topic? If there is more than one goal, list them in order of importance, i.e., primary, secondary, other.
3. Does the goal of the current topic align with the goal of the educational ministry/program?
4. What is the desired outcome of engaging in the current topic? If there is more than one, list them all.
5. Does the desired outcome align with the goal of the educational ministry/program? Answer this question for each stated outcome.
6. Is each outcome passive or active? (Refer to the examples provided earlier in the Sunday morning adult education class discussion.) Again, answer this for each stated outcome.

■ Why answer these questions for at least three teaching-learning routines of your congregation? Because multiples provide for insights that are more revealing than single cases. We tend to make assumptions about many practices in the church. Completing an inventory such as this puts the assumptions right out in front and allows for a reality check across this whole segment of the church's life.

■ Back to the exercise! Gather the data you've collected regarding the teaching-learning routines of your local church setting. You'll need to be able to "look across" the information, so put the data into a form that makes sense to you and that could be shared with others easily. When I do consultations and learning events with various conferences, associations, or local churches, I tell the participants, "I'll give you a format you may use, but if a different format makes more sense to you, use it instead." What's important here is that you get the data into some useful visual form because you are going to be comparing and contrasting the data across the various ministries and programs.

I favor matrices, so I'd create one in which I could record and review the data gathered. You can find a sample matrix already set up and ready for your use at www.thepilgrimpress.com. Because I favor compiling information by hand, often writing it out on paper then transcribing it to print form, I rarely begin with anything as neatly constructed as the matrix on www.thepilgrimpress.com. But I have colleagues and two sons who are so tech-savvy that they go right to the computer for everything. Do what works for you. Again, what's important is that you get the data into some useful visual form so you can compare and contrast the data across the various ministries and programs.

▉ We come now to the point in your assessing process where you ask yourself/yourselves these questions:

1. Do these teaching-learning routines stimulate, foster, support and sustain adult Christian formation or might they unintentionally truncate it?

2. If they stimulate, foster, support and sustain adult Christian formation, how do they do that and how do you know they do that?

3. If they do not stimulate, foster, support and sustain Christian formation of the adult participants and leaders, how do you know they don't and what's missing?

4. Are these teaching-learning routines purposeful, under-purposed, or un-purposed?

▉ Make notes of your discoveries, insights, ideas, and even brick walls into which you run. All can be helpful.

As you undertake this Point-in-Time Exercise, take a moment to consider two practical issues: the need to exercise diplomacy and the need to resist what I call the "finite trap." Regarding diplomacy, whenever there are established programs about which individuals feel passionately, the wise leader — laity or clergy — invites the participants of those programs to conduct a self-assessment and suggest, for example, ways they would like to enhance Christian faith formation within that program. When assessment of activities and programs across the life of the congregation takes place concurrently, and with the active involvement of the participants, the assessment is less likely to be interpreted as a hostile takeover attempt. Regarding the "finite trap," it has at least two characteristics. Congregations and their leaders repeatedly trip over thinking that (1) there can only be one of something, for example the Women's Bible Study, and that (2) the "something" is a one-size-fits all. One-size-fits-all rarely works in clothing — men's, women's, adolescents', or children's — and it rarely works in local congregations. As for multiple activities and programs around the same topic, for example Bible study for women, so long as the groups remain in keeping with the mission and vision of the church and so long as they welcome newcomers, then the more the merrier.

Christian Formation is Process, not Product

Earlier in the chapter I stated that faith and its companion discipleship do not come about through a banking model, but that formation of Christian adults is process — process that equips and nurtures in the here-and-now, plus process that will re-equip and re-nurture throughout the adult Christian life. I want to add that formation of Christian adults is both organic and intentional.

Sondra Higgins Matthaei offers a description of faith formation that I find helpful. She writes that faith formation is

> our participation in God's work of inviting persons into relation-ship with God, self, others, and creation. . . . The faith communi-ty's role in this process is to participate in God's work by creating an intentional process of developing identity and vocation within [the Christian] tradition.[8]

Matthaei goes on to clarify what she means by Christian identity and Christian vocation.

> I have defined Christian identity as coming to know oneself as a Christian, having assimilated the values, beliefs, and lifestyle of one who professes to be a follower of Jesus Christ. . . . And Christian vocation is the response one makes to God's grace — the discipleship of loving God and all of God's creation, including our neighbors.[9]

What, then, is the aim of faith formation? Matthaei suggests it is two-fold: (1) "deepening relationship with God," i.e., spirituality, and (2) "the faithful witness through word and action that grows out of this relationship."[10] It is through individuals' deepening relationship with God that they experience transformation from lives focused elsewhere to lives of "loving God's creation, including oneself and others".[11]

Look at the process-oriented words in Matthaei's description of Christian faith formation.

- participation, (God's) work, inviting, relationship
- role, participate, (God's) work creating, developing, identity, vocation. coming to know
- response, discipleship, loving

There is nothing static here. Even identity and vocation are not truly products, somehow identified and solidified once and for all. While Christian identity defines us and shapes us, it is also defined, shaped, and challenged by the relationships and life events we continue to encounter as a part of living. Similarly, Christian vocation, by definition response and discipleship, defines and shapes directions we take and choices we make while being refined and reshaped by the realities and consequences of actually loving God, loving all God's creation, and loving our "neighbors" in deed as well as word.

At the end of the Point-in-Time Exercise "What's in Your Teaching-Learning Routine?" you encountered this series of questions.

1. Do these teaching-learning routines stimulate, foster, support and sustain adult Christian formation or do they unintentionally truncate it?

2. If they stimulate, foster, support and sustain adult Christian formation, how do they do that and how do you know they do that?

3. If they do not stimulate, foster, support and sustain Christian formation of the adult participants and leaders, how do you know they don't and what's missing?

4. Are these teaching-learning routines purposeful, under-purposed, or un-purposed?

Even earlier in the chapter I stated that there can be potential for otherwise un-purposed or under-purposed educational ministries to be transformed to formative ministries of adult Christians, and promised to return to this a little later in the chapter. Here it is.

Point-in-Time Exercise: Purposing for Formative Ministry

■ Review the answers generated in response to questions 1–4 in the "What's in Your Teaching-Learning Routine?" Point-in-Time Exercise.

- Select one of the teaching-learning routines or ministries identified as under-purposed or un-purposed.
- List ideas about the kind of stated purpose that would be needed in order for that routine or ministry to better foster the continuing faith formation of the adults involved.
- Select one stated purpose idea from the list. If a group is working together, they need to select a single purpose idea.
- Identify several steps to take — and how those steps will be taken — in order to integrate that stated purpose into that particular ministry.
- Decide on a period of time to "live into" the repurposed ministry as well as when and how to evaluate effectiveness. Use any of the questions/ assessment ideas you encountered earlier in the chapter.
- Put the repurposing into action.

We're Off and Running

As this first chapter comes to a close, look at the groundwork you've done already toward adult faith formation. Vital congregations are those willing to do self-assessment, visioning and repurposing, as well as get-our-hands-dirty work. Intentionally accepting our roles and responsibilities when it comes to Christian faith formation of adults — whether of old-timers to the church or brand new-timers to the church, its Christ, and its faith — we'll be going places in ourselves and in company with others we would most likely not have gone otherwise.

Welcome to the race worth running, and the course worthy of our energies.

Two

What Does It Mean
to Understand Curriculum
as Faith Formation?

I **remember the evening quite well. I was in a local United Church of Christ at the request of the senior minister, a colleague and friend.** He'd asked me to come spend a session helping his committee leaders get a start using the new *Seasons of the Spirit Congregational Life* curricular resource. We'd worked together before and both knew the value of a consultant's leadership when bringing people on board with new ideas. The Christian Education Committee had selected *Seasons of the Spirit* for the church's Sunday educational ministry programs and my colleague was excited about the resource's focus on engaging the whole life of the church.

We gathered in one of the church's meeting areas: the Director of Christian Education, the Mission and Outreach Committee and Worship Committee chairpersons, the pastor and me. I checked in with them to see what familiarity they had with *Seasons of the Spirit Congregational Life*. They each had a copy of it. Several had leafed through it, several had read a little of it. Not a lot of familiarity overall yet. I walked us through the resource together, providing a roadmap for the layout of *Congregational*

Life, pointing out where they could find topic-specific information, such as liturgy and worship ideas, mission and outreach sections, the biblical background sections focusing on the lectionary readings of each Sunday, the educational ministry themes and interconnections with the lectionary. It's always a little overwhelming to discover so many possibilities within one resource, but so far so good.

Then I asked this experienced group of lay leaders to think across worship, education, and service. "Imagine," I said, "how the three could tie in with one another right here in this church's life." The lay leaders looked at me. I tried again, different words, same basic idea.

You could see the wheels turning, each thinking very hard. But the simple reality was, as further conversation revealed, these highly motivated and skilled leaders were confounded by the challenge of thinking and planning holistically for the life of the church so that worship, education, mission and service would be no longer discrete entities with discrete tasks but instead mutually energizing, reinforcing, and interconnected. In other words, so that worship, education, mission and service were together the curriculum of the church and by extension faith formation.

Ask a Christian religious educator what Christian education is, and she or he will respond, "Everything in the church is Christian education." The same can be said of faith formation. Yet within the overall leadership of the church — clergy and lay — Christian education is treated much the same as Mark Twain remarked about the weather: "Everyone talks about it, but no one does anything about it."

The challenge is two-fold. (1) Not to nod our heads, "Yes, Christian education is everything in the church," and thereby trivialize it into virtual nothingness — that is to say nothing of any significance to the full life and mission, i.e., the "real work" of the church. (2) Respond "It is?! Show me! Let me see what you see!" and thereby enter into the creative and powerfully transformative acts, processes and dynamics by which faith is formed, shaped, nurtured, sustained, deepened, set on fire, and turned loose in the furthering of God's realm. Wow!

One goal of this chapter is to move you, the reader, from wherever you may be regarding Christian religious education and its Siamese twin, faith formation, in the church to "It is?! Show me! Let me see what you see!"

Let's begin with the following exercise. Write down the first five words that come to mind when you hear or read the word "curriculum." Do that now, right in the margin if nowhere else.

When I ask this question at workshops, conferences, and local church gatherings the responses most often include:

Sunday school materials
confirmation program materials
Bible Quest
Seasons of the Spirit
The Present Word
Workshop Rotation materials
Vacation Bible School
Kerygma
Discipleship
Power Express
Logos
Lectionary based
Bible-story based
age specific
intergenerational

Do you see any of your words on this list? If so, it's not surprising. The tendency is to equate curriculum with the actual resources, be they print, audio-visual or computer-based — lesson plans, learner and teacher guides, posters and CDs. There's good reason for the tendency, since the resource creators and publishers classify their products as "curriculum," as do most pastors and volunteer teachers in local churches. Nonetheless, to equate curriculum with curricular resources only is like equating the sport of football with playbooks and televised games or to equate the world of cooking with cookbooks and cooking shows.

The term curriculum comes from the Latin *currere*. *Currere* means "to run," as in "to run the course."[1] Imagine a race course or a cross-country course and the runners "running the course," and you'll have the basis for a fuller understanding of curriculum as the course to be run. An authentic question to ask then is: what *is* the curriculum of the church? If it's not the resources we use, what's left? The answer is: The whole of the church's life provides the curricula, the courses to be run.

In her book *Fashion Me a People*, Maria Harris provides us with a portrait of the early church's first curriculum. She calls attention to the book called The Acts of the Apostles in the New Testament, particularly the following portions of chapter two.[2]

[32] This Jesus God raised up, and of that all of us are witnesses
. . . [42] They devoted themselves to the apostles' teaching and fellowship, to the breaking of bread and the prayers. . . [44] All who
believed were together and had all things in common; [45]they
would sell their possessions and goods and distribute the pro-
ceeds to all, as any had need. [46] Day by day, as they spent much
time together in the temple, they broke bread at home and ate
their food with glad and generous hearts, [47] praising God and
having the goodwill of all the people. And day by day the Lord
added to their number those who were being saved. (Acts 2:32,
42, 44–47.)

Harris identified in Luke's account of these earliest church activities "the central elements, or the set of forms, that embody the course of the church's life
. . ."[3] There are five: *kerygma, didache, leiturgia , koinonia*, and *diakonia*.
Kerygma is the curriculum of proclamation, of "proclaiming the word of
Jesus' resurrection." *Didache* is the curriculum of teaching, and includes the
"activity of teaching." *Leiturgia* is the curriculum of prayer. It is "coming
together to pray and to re-present Jesus in the breaking of bread." *Koinonia*
is the curriculum of community, and is far more than simply fellowship. It is
the way of being in community with one another that is uniquely Christian.
Diakonia is the curriculum of service, of "caring for those in need."[4]

Here then is the life of the congregation. Harris proposes that "fashioning and refashioning of this set of forms" which are the life of a congregation
"is the core of the educational ministry of the church."[5]

Point-in-Time Exercise: A Little Taste of the Possible

▓ For this exercise, a worksheet is provided at www.thepilgrimpress.com for
your use. Expand it as needed, or create one of your own.

- Make a list of those programs, events, activities, ministries going well
  at your church that are not explicitly *didache* (teaching). These are the
  things about which you and the congregation would say, "We do this
  well" and feel good about.
- Look back on your list. Select one.
- Ask yourself, "How could this program, event, activity, ministry be transformed into more intentional faith formation?"

- Write your ideas! The thinking and creative process is strengthened incredibly when you put pen to paper.
- Look back over your written ideas. Ask yourself, "What have I discovered through doing this activity?" Jot down your responses. Yes, put them into written form.
- If you are doing this exercise within a group, discuss your event and your discoveries with one other person.
- If you did the exercise on your own, seek out a colleague and discuss your event and discoveries with her or him. Consider lunch or coffee together. Fill your colleague in on what you've been reading, and the discussion will be even more fruitful.

Stories from the Field

At a day-long conference for clergy and church educators, the participants went through the exercise described above. After discussion in pairs I invited them to share their examples with the group as a whole. One man stood up, identifying himself as a local church pastor, and mentioned several programs the congregation does well. He said he focused on the church's men's softball team because, "Well, just because I did."

"I'll never look at it [the men's softball team] the same way again," he said. He went on to explain that he hadn't figured out exactly how to work the shift so the softball team program integrated intentional faith formation, but he was challenged and energized by the possibilities.

At a different seminar, about twenty clergy and laity worked at the same task. When they shared discoveries with the whole group, a number of possibilities as well as self-discoveries were candidly reported. One retired pastor told of a group of veterans with which he is involved. The group's participants were members of the local church who came together for mutual support, and they included the whole span from World War II and the Korean War to the Vietnam War, then to the Persian Gulf, Afghanistan, and Iraq Wars. The pastor, a former military chaplain, reflected on the men's struggle with the horrors of war, what they'd had to do as soldiers and sailors, how the edges of that brokenness had never really been healed. He said, "Now I understand the power of the healing I can bring into the group. I've sat with the men and they struggle together on critical questions of where was God in all this awfulness. There was this need of cleansing, forgiveness and renewal they longed for. After thinking about the group through this process, I get that I can bring them the words and the rituals of our faith that can become sources for that cleansing, that forgiveness, that renewal."

Context and Texts of Faith Formation

The whole life of the congregation, indeed the life of the church as the body of Christ, is the context and the "texts" of faith formation. Clergy are good at exegeting biblical texts. What we need to practice is exegeting the life of the local congregation and fashioning ministry from and to it.

I am in no way suggesting that clergy narrowly focus on only the congregation's life as it exists at the moment so as to channel all their efforts into sustaining that single body of believers. I am suggesting that much of what constitutes the life of a congregation is kept isolated, even insulated, from faith formative dynamics and practices. Further, I am suggesting that starting "local" makes the starting concrete and manageable, and therefore more enticing.

Re-Envisioning the Course and Its Running

Let's return to the linguistic roots of curriculum again. *Currer* means "to run," as in "to run the course." Imagine the course you see before you is a closed one, like a high school track or soccer field. Now imagine discovering that running is not limited to the closed course. Imagine discovering that, in fact, very little running is actually done within a closed course. Imagine running as the movie character Forrest Gump implicitly understood and explicitly experienced it: he ran wherever his running took him.

Indeed, running takes place just about anywhere and for any number of reasons. Running comes naturally to children and can remain important throughout an entire life. Running can take you to places of enjoyment, get you away from threatening situations, move you into danger in order to protect or rescue another, free you from stress, sustain health and vigor, and energize your whole being.

In my roles as a United Church Education Consultant and member of a college faculty, I get to work with men and women seeking training and education in Christian religious education. Some are local church educators serving in congregations who want formal course work in Christian education in order to better fulfill their call. Some are traditional-age college students preparing to be directors of Christian education or to enter seminary in preparation for ordained ministry. Some are regulars in the lay academies of various conferences. In the beginning, they all have an initial understanding of what Christian education and faith formation is.

Christian education begins with instruction on the beliefs, values, and practices of the faith community. This encompasses, but is not limited to, teaching the Bible in Sunday school or small Bible study groups, family prayer or worship time, and Wednesday night programs.[6]

Religious instruction is primarily based on developing one's faith and moral values and guiding individuals through their lives by showing them the different aspects of life.[7]

Then we explore the work of Maria Harris. They get their first glimpse at the scope of faith formation and educational ministries. In class or workshop they wrestle with Thomas Groome's intimidating writing style, mining the rich, dense text for golden nuggets.[8] They discover one of Groome's nuggets: that Christian religious education is a political activity.

Educational activity with pilgrims in time is a political activity. I understand political activity to be any deliberate and structured intervention in people's lives which attempts to influence how they live their lives in society. . . . Christian religious education is a political activity with pilgrims in time that deliberately and intentionally attends with them to the activity of God in our present, to the Story of the Christian faith community, and to the Vision of God's Kingdom, the seeds of which are already among us.

They encounter Roger Shinn's conviction that reconciliation is the one ministry of the church, and that three tasks are needed for this ministry of reconciliation.

Within the ministry of reconciliation . . . three tasks mutually reinforce and correct each other . . . incorporation in the life of the faith community, appropriation of a [faith] heritage, and training in mission. More important than their mutual distinction is their interpenetration. Isolation and undue emphasis on any one may falsify Christian faith.[9]

By the end of the workshop, conference, or class, the participants' understanding of Christian education and faith formation has transformed.

Christian education is building a person's walk with God through religious education, worship, personal reflection, service, and praise.[10]

It seems that somewhere along the way, I had gotten the idea in my head that education simply stopped at a certain point. There was no real basis for it, no definite age, but somewhere around early adulthood. Looking back on that theory now I see it as rather ridiculous. Christian education is all inclusive and encompasses every facet of the believer's life, from Baptism to Sunday School to Confirmation, through Marriage, and finally into old age. . . . There is no point in which a Christian simply graduates and stops learning. . . . [Christian education] is not limited to any one part of a person's life, but rather it is the backbone in their life.[11]

Christian education is the process of developing one's faith and moral values; developing a greater Biblical knowledge and knowledge of one's own church; developing a greater sense of the process and application of critical thinking; while at all times keeping in mind the ultimate challenge of balancing the need for constant change in life and the need for stability in life.[12]

Suddenly Christian education is no longer limited to a circumscribed track, but opens in every direction. Possibilities not yet articulated sweeten the air. Vistas not yet in full clarity delight the view. I witness eyes brightening, faces opening, new energies radiating. Individuals — clergy or laity or student — often sit back in their seats and simply breathe, as if windows had been thrown open and fresh air blew in. Others write as quickly as they can, to catch the insights flooding in. It is a Lazarus moment.[13] Called from the confines of tomb-sized assumptions and limits, they are unbound, set free, newly alive.

Point-in-Time Exercise:
The Ministry Menu of _____
(name of your church)

■ This exercise provides you and your congregation with an interesting perspective on the range of ministries as well as the range or lack of range of leaders. It also provides an interesting perspective on the range and level of participation across Harris' five forms in this particular congregation's setting.

■ List the activities, programs, ministries of your congregation, placing each under the "form" it best fits. For the website worksheet, I've included Maria Harris' description of each form for ease of reference. Think through an entire year if you really want to come up with as complete a list as possible.

■ Now mark those you lead, those that others lead, those in which you are a participant but not the leader, and those in which others are participants not leaders. Use whatever symbols or shorthand is useful for you.

■ These are a portion of the in-house "texts" of your congregation. Vital congregations grow ministries based on the mission and vision of the church *and* the faith-based passions of the congregants. Vital congregations multiply leadership pools. Vital congregations would not expect the pastor to be an alpha leader, but rather a senior partner in a multi-person leadership cadre.

■ Look over your list again.

- What patterns do you see?
- What positives are already present?
- What's neglected?
- What seems in-grown or perpetuating without clear, vibrant purpose?
- Which activities/programs/ministries intersect across forms? Which stand alone?
- Which activities/programs/ministries would be recognizable as contexts of faith formation as they currently occur? In what ways?

Hold on to this information. It is your local church's Ministry Menu and therefore it contains some of the texts available for exegeting. You will need these for use with the next Point-in-Time Exercise.

Faith Formation, Multiple Intelligences, Learning Cone and Course Running

You can't just talk at people if you want them to grow in their faith formation and discipleship. It may be very satisfying for a pastor or lay leader, but it won't move people forward in their faith.

39

Activities just for the sake of "doing something" or "making it fun" are not the answer either. To paraphrase John Dewey, all learning is experiential, but not all experiences are learning. What's a pastor or lay leader to do?

Bear with me while I interject discussion of Howard Gardner's and Edgar Dale's insights into learning. I promise to connect these with faith formation as I go along.

Multiple Intelligences

Some of you may be familiar with Howard Gardner's research and theory of multiple intelligences. For those who are not, I will give a brief overview. If you wish to explore multiple intelligences more there are several sources you could use. If you are web savvy, do an online search for helpful websites. Public libraries most likely have at least basic information.

If the educational ministry of a church in your area is using a rotational model, ask for any information they have on Gardner's multiple intelligences. If you have school teachers in your congregation, ask them for whatever information they have. There is a growing bank of information addressing early childhood through adolescence relative to creating learning environments and plans that take into account the multiple intelligences of individuals. Basic educational psychology text books include information on Gardner's theory as well, so inquiring at a used textbook store or online site could produce an inexpensive copy.

In his 1983 work *Frames of Mind: The Theory of Multiple Intelligences,* Howard Gardner initially identified seven discreet abilities or excellences through which we do our thinking and learning.[14] He called them intelligences and named them linguistic, logical-mathematical, musical, kinesthetic, spatial, interpersonal, and intrapersonal. Jerry Larsen highlighted four of Gardner's discoveries in his book, *Religious Education and the Brain. A Practical Resource for Understanding How We Learn about God*:

- We can excel in at least seven ways of thinking: linguistic, logical-mathematical, musical, kinesthetic, spatial, interpersonal, and intrapersonal.
- These seven ways represent seven different intelligences in human cognition. Everyone has these cognitive abilities in varying strengths.
- Very few people are excellent at every one of them. All seven, however, represent the range of thought processes, information and skills that roughly

define the human repertoire.

- In other words, the seven intelligences describe the range of human excellence. They help define us.[15]

Larsen helps us understand some of the interplay between these multiple intelligences, faith formation and faith expression. Below are excerpts from Larsen's chapter "The Sevenfold Path to Religious Intelligence."[16] In them, Larsen offers glimpses of how the various multiple intelligences manifest themselves within our more familiar religious contexts. His examples are not meant to be exhaustive, simply suggestive.

- "In religious life, [linguistic] intelligence serves us as we read scripture, talk and write our religious pilgrimages, learn to read ancient languages, do research, create poetry and prayers, and listen to the words of others."[17]
- "[Spatial intelligence] makes it possible for us to express meanings, faith, events and stories in the graphic arts."[18]
- "We call on our musical intelligence when we sing songs about or faith, use musical instruments to set a mood, or transform an environment."[19]
- "Faith seeks understanding. Making sense of our affirmations requires the skills of logic, integration and inquiry. When we do theology, philosophy, and the pursuit of our curiosities, we are using [logical-mathematical] intelligence."[20]
- "We use our [body] kinesthetic abilities in the faith community when we participate in ceremonies and liturgies that require gestures and postures. We use them when faith is expressed in dance or movement. [Body] kinesthetic intelligence is involved in dramatic recreations of our faith stories, and in the gestures we use when we greet, nurture and converse with each other."[21]
- "It takes a special kind of intelligence to live in community and covenant with others. At its core is an awareness of the commonalities and unique-nesses that exist among people who live in *troth*. [Interpersonal intelligence] shows itself as friendship, love, respect, understanding and sensitivity."[22]
- "Traditionally, [intrapersonal intelligence] helps us pray, meditate, confess, experience gratitude and need, dread and joy. If one of the results of a religious journey is being transformed (we use words like 'born again,' 'saved,' 'redeemed,' 'found,' 'welcomed home,' 'enlightened' — depending on our tradition), then this intelligence too is central to our religious life."[23]

Several other interesting characteristics about the multiple intelligences are worth our attention at this point. One is that, though everyone has all the intelligences and everyone's abilities vary in strength depending on the individual, even people with the same strong intelligences experience them in combinations unique to themselves. A colleague of mine once helped make this point using her three children as examples. All three had strong kinesthetic and musical intelligences. Encouraged by their parents to pursue their individual interests and talents, the son manifested his kinesthetic and musical intelligences in his expertise with hand bells. One twin daughter's kinesthetic and musical intelligences manifested themselves in vocal music and dance. The other twin daughter's kinesthetic and musical intelligences manifested themselves in instrumental music and marching band.

A second interesting characteristic of the intelligences is that those in which we are strongest give us the greatest pleasure and sense of fulfillment when we are able to exercise them regularly. This was vividly illustrated in the educational lives of children who attended a school where the curriculum took seriously the children's multiple intelligences. All the children in this elementary school spent the first period of the day in a class that exercised their strongest intelligence. For some it was vocal music through choir, for others it was band. For some it was advanced math, for others creative writing or science research and experiments. For some it was group projects, for some it was individual project work. As the children progressed through the rest of their day they had to use their other intelligences to learn the regular school subjects. Students reported how energized they were after getting to start the day in their "favorite" class. Visitors to the school commented on how all the students were gifted students. But the students were not the "gifted" students of the town. They were randomly selected from the general enrollment of the local public school district. It seemed that they had all learned to excel through the learning environment that took Gardner's theory of multiple intelligences seriously, and not just in their strongest area.[24]

A third interesting characteristic is that the intelligences which are our "weakest" can be developed. They will likely never be as strong as our primary intelligences, but they can be strengthened and therefore can be drawn upon more fully for our thinking and learning.

There is a wonderful scene in the movie *Chariots of Fire*, when Eric Liddell, a runner who was also a missionary, assures his sister, "I believe God made me for a purpose. He also made me *fast*. And when I run I feel His pleasure."[25] The runner understands his ability to run is a God-given gift. He accepts it as a gift, and in that acceptance and his willingness to use that gift to its maximum capacity running becomes an authentic spiritual experience for him. Perhaps what the early church recognized as spiritual gifts and fruits of the spirit were manifestations of multiple intelligences: God-given, vibrant abilities called forth and nurtured by the faith community for the purpose of serving God, God's people, and all who had need.

Learning Cone

Edgar Dale's research into people's learning resulted in some interesting findings. Again some of you may be familiar with his work either by name or by concept. Dale found it useful to illustrate his findings through a diagram he called the Cone of Learning.[26] The Cone is represented by a triangle cut through by horizontal lines. The lines mark out percentages of what we tend to remember after, for instance, two weeks depending on how we were involved with the information. If you are internet-savvy, you can find numerous versions of Dale's Cone of Learning. One version has also been placed on the website for this book at www.thepilgrimpress.com. Or you can sketch one based on the discussion below. Start at the top of the triangle and draw a horizontal line for each percentage mentioned.

What do we tend to remember after two weeks? Not very much if we only read, hear, or see the information. The percents for information only read, only heard, and only seen are, respectively, 10%, 20%, and 30%. Even when hearing and seeing are combined, it only results in a 50% rate of remembering. Dale described these lowest percentage performers as verbal and visual receiving, and identified them as *passive* involvement. If you've ever wondered why your words of wisdom or warning seem to fall on deaf ears — your children's, your co-workers, the church council members, the congregation on Sunday morning or Saturday evening — it's more than likely the result of passive involvement on the part of those "receiving" your words.

Much better remembering occurs when we become actively involved with the information at hand. We tend to remember 70% of what we ourselves say in roles of responsibility or active participation, and nearly 100% of what we say and do. Dale calls these involvements receiving/participating and doing, and identifies them as *active* involvement.

It's no wonder that a local church stewardship committee I once staffed underwent profound transformation of their concept and response to Christian stewardship over a year's time. They were *actively* involved. During the meetings they each told their stories of why church was important to them and how they had experienced faith in God and Jesus Christ. They studied stewardship materials, including biblical and theological underpinnings, from their denomination. They planned ways to connect the congregation with what they were discovering, and fulfilled those plans throughout the year. As the annual "financial campaign" came near, they candidly and with great care told one another of having rethought everything about their giving and the significant changes they were making in their lives in order to reflect holistic stewardship.

It's no wonder children of a congregation can retell and re-enact the story of Jesus' birth from a young age. They are the ones often "saying" the narrative's lines and "doing" what Mary and Joseph, the shepherds, angels, magi, sometimes even the sheep and donkey did.

It's no wonder I've included Point-in-Time Exercises throughout this book!

Multiple intelligences + Cone of Learning

Jerry Larsen's *Religious Education and the Brain* provides a diagram that helps us look at the multiple intelligences and the cone of learning together.[27] You can find the diagram at www.thepilgrimpress.com or sketch one like this: Draw seven columns of graduated heights. The tallest column, which forms the centerpiece of the diagram, represents verbal intelligence. To the left and right sides of that middle column are two slightly shorter columns, respectively spatial intelligence and logical-mathematical intelligence. Flanking those two columns are two more, again slightly shorter: interpersonal on the left, intrapersonal on the right. Finally there are two, shortest, columns: kinesthetic on the left and musical on the right.

Point in Time Exercise: What's on Your Learning Cone?

▓ Time to put these models to use for your congregational setting. Using the list you generated for your Ministry Menu in the previous Point-in-Time Exercise, place each ministry/activity/program into one of the Learning Cone categories. For example, if you listed collecting nonperishable food for a local food pantry, you might place it in the "What we say and do" category of "Doing the real thing." Certainly for those who remember to bring the food, it's "doing." What about those who hear the announcement at church or read it in the bulletin, newsletter or website but don't remember to bring in the food even though they would bring food in if they did remember? Perhaps that's a question better left for another time.

▨ Once you have assigned the various ministries/activities/programs to a category in Dale's learning cone, estimate the percentage of the total represented by each category's list. For example, if "hearing words" has twelve of the total 36 programs/ministries/activities you identified, then its portion is about 33 %. Sketch out a triangle that illustrates those percentages. Keep the categories in the same order as in Dale's learning cone, but vary the size of each category depending on the percent it is used in the life of your congregation.

▨ As you look at the diagram you've sketched, what do you notice? I'm a firm believer in the power of human beings to make meaning out of all sorts of information, and to uncover insights they would not otherwise have discerned. So, take some time to process what's there to be noticed. However, if you'd like a little assistance seeing the forest for the trees, try any or all of the prompts below.

- Which types of involvement occur most often, passive or active? Who's involved with those as leaders? As participants? What insights can you glean from that?
- Which types of involvement are least frequent, passive or active? Again, who's involved with those as leaders? As participants? What insights can you glean from that?
- Are there any patterns between ministries/programs/activities listed within specific forms (*koinonia*, *kerygma*, *diakonia*, *leiturgia*, *didache*) and the types of involvement of those ministries/programs/activities? What might that suggest?

▨ At this point, let's bring in the multiple intelligences. Sketch over the top of your congregation's learning cone diagram Larsen's vertical diagram of the multiple intelligences (see above). What do you notice now?

- Which multiple intelligence abilities are called upon most often? Who's involved with the corresponding activities/programs/ministries as leaders? As participants? What insights can you glean from that?

- Which multiple intelligence abilities are involved least frequently? Again, who's involved with the corresponding activities/programs/ministries as leaders? As participants? What insights can you glean from that?
- Are there any patterns between ministries/programs/activities listed within specific forms (*koinonia, kerygma, diakonia, leiturgia, didache*) and the types of multiple intelligences included in those ministries/ programs/activities? What might that suggest?

Jesus' Teaching and Dale's Learning Cone

What Edgar Dale helps us realize through his Learning Cone is that we can tap into powerful formation tools by paying attention to realities of human learning. What Howard Gardner helps us realize through his work with multiple intelligences is that we humans have a variety of conduits for faith formation, all of which are valuable, all of which are present in each person, but none of which is the primary conduit for everyone.

What the biblical narratives help us realize is that faith formation was never primarily by passive involvement. Although oral tradition had a significant role to play, the narratives were based on the experiences of individuals and groups in relationship with God, experiences that were, by their very nature, active involvement. Rituals marking the faith life of the community were re-enactments imbued with the tactile, sensory participation for all involved: bitter herbs, salt water, roast lamb to experience again the night of escape from Egypt; bread and wine to experience again the Last Supper and the presence of the living Christ.

Prophets, desperate to get the nation's leaders and populace to pay attention to the radical rupture occurring between their ways of doing business and God's role for God's people, dramatized the prophetic word. One walked down the streets of Jerusalem with his neck in a heavy wooden ox yoke, simulating the yoke of oppression Israel would live under because of the nation's rulers' misdeeds. Another dug a hole in an earthen wall and in the darkness of night, crawled through it and dragged his baggage after him, as one would who is going into exile, all to simulate the exile of Israel coming at the hands of the Babylonians.

The disciples of Jesus walked everywhere with him, saw him heal men, women, and children, got first-hand scoldings, observed his way with people of each social and religious class and stratum, wrestled with and were tutored in parables they couldn't figure out themselves, tried their own hands at healing and proclaiming that God's Realm was breaking forth right now, grieved beyond measure as Jesus died on a Roman executioner's cross, and couldn't believe their eyes or ears when they first learned of the resurrection. When the time came for them to emerge from hiding, they had a faith formed from all those experiences, successes, failures, and vivid memories. Ignited by the Holy Spirit, they created environments where others could catch the fire of faith in a crucified and risen Christ, experience a faith transformed, and literally live out the effects of that transformation through service, fellowship, learning, passing along the word of Jesus' resurrection, prayer, and re-presenting Jesus in the breaking of bread together.

Faith formation is experience-based. Look at Sondra Higgins Matthaei's description again:

> Faith formation [is] our participation in God's work of inviting persons into relationship with God, self, others, and creation. . . . The faith community's role in this process is to participate in God's work by creating an intentional process of developing identity and vocation within [the Christian] tradition.[28]

Notice the experiential words and the active words in Matthaei's description: participation, relationship, process, inviting, participate, creating, and developing.

Not all experiences are faith-formative even if they are brought to us by the church. Therefore, it is essential, it is critical that we pay attention to the experiences of individuals and create means and ministries that bridge from "just experiences" to faith-formative experiences. As we've seen in this chapter, we have a far better chance of accomplishing this faith-filled goal if we think and plan for active involvement instead of relying on words, words and more words.

Time Out for Rest

Time to take a breather. If you've been completing the Point-in-Time Exercises — I certainly hope you have, since that's much more active involvement than simply reading through the words — you have garnered a significant amount of information all of which is directly grounded in your congregational context. You've also been "making meaning" of the information generated by the Point-in-Time Exercises. I invite you to read back through your summation or reflection sections of each Point-in-Time Exercise. These are the sections when you considered questions such as "What patterns do you see?" and "What do you notice?" Then, for a little while, simply put it away. Don't flush it out of your brain! Just let it rest, like good bread dough is set aside to rest before it's given its final shape and form.

Earlier in this chapter I suggested that the entire life of the congregation is the curriculum of faith formation. I suggested that the activities, programs, and ministries you listed and categorized using Maria Harris' five forms of a congregation's life (*koinonia, kerygma, diakonia, eiturgia, didache*) are a portion of the in-house "texts" of your congregation, and that what we need to practice is exegeting these in-house "texts" and fashioning ministry from them. We also need to recognize that there are, in fact, many more in-house "texts" not yet discovered within the lives of those already part of the congregation, as well as "texts" not yet discovered — or at least not yet exegeted — in the communities beyond the local church itself. All that being said, you have in your hands by way of the Point-in-Time Exercises of this chapter good, trustworthy texts into which you and your church leaders can dig more deeply — can exegete most enthusiastically — so as to hear more clearly and engage more intentionally God's word for faith formation across and within the whole life of the congregation.

I encourage you to exegete and implement well.

Three

Parents et al.: Re-establishing Homes of Faith and Formation

A word about the word parent. . . Families and households come in all manner of configurations, and parenting roles are filled not only by biological and adoptive parents, but also by grandparents, aunts, uncles, older siblings, cousins, step-parents and step-siblings, heterosexual couples, lesbian and gay couples, single moms, single dads, foster families and legal guardians. Sometimes members of a local church fill the role of parent for children and youth whose home lives are in crisis, unstable, or geographically distant, even if no official status is given to those loving, care-giving church members. Throughout this book and especially in this chapter I mean for the term *parent* to capture all those relational possibilities and any unintentionally left unnamed.

O nce upon a time, not so long ago, local churches were filled with families of all shapes and sizes every Sunday morning. Parents brought well behaved children for hour-long Sunday School and stayed for their own adult classes. Pews filled up for worship: mothers and fathers and children sat quietly and respectfully together, grandparents or neighbors sat nearby. Friendly greetings were exchanged between all. Since everyone knew everyone else, visitors were easily recognized and warmly made to feel welcome. Parents of infants automatically moved from the sanctuary to the Cry Room if the little one became fussy. Toddlers and young grade-schoolers patiently stared at the plain backs of the pews ahead of them without kicking the hymnal racks, banging their heels on the wood or squirming in their seats. Older children paid attention to the printed bulletin, sang from the hymnal, did not fidget or whisper during the prayers, perhaps drew quietly during the sermon, never poked a sibling or otherwise caused a disturbance. No one left the sanctuary just to go to the bathroom or get a drink of water, especially the children. After eighteen years of attending Sunday School and worship, the now-grown children took on tasks within the church as responsible adult members, bringing in time first spouses and then children to Sunday School and worship without missing a beat.

In this time, not so long ago, there were always enough Sunday School teachers, most of them parents of children in the Sunday School, and these teachers used the week to prepare their classes' lessons. They did not wait till Saturday night or Sunday morning to pick up the curriculum resources. In this time, not so long ago, there were enough energetic and dedicated young adults or parents to be youth group leaders. There were enough volunteers for special events, church suppers work days, fund raisers, committees and boards. In this time, not so long ago, parents did not drop children off for Sunday School; they came in and participated in adult education and then stayed for worship as a family. In this time, once upon a time, not so long ago.

When I'm invited to consult with a church or lead a workshop I hear a lot of this kind of talk about the good old days. I hear a lot of reasons why the church (i.e., "my church") is struggling (i.e., there's not enough money, people, volunteers, dedicated people, workers, giving. . .). Much of the blame is directed at The Parents, and by association The Children and The Youth. The complaints are numerous. The children watch too much television, play too many computer and video games, talk and text too much on their cell phones. They spend too much time and money going to movies, buying DVDs and CDs, and shopping at the mall for iPods and bling. The children and youth wear inappropriate clothes; they behave badly and have bad manners. They are in too many organized sports and other activities. If they are teens they have after-school jobs. All these children and youth are overindulged, have far too much discretionary money, and only want to be entertained. It's the parents' fault. It's also the public school and community leadership's fault, because no longer is Wednesday evening protected as "church night."

Though repeated and vigorous, this blaming and fault-finding has yet, to my knowledge, been able to produce positive results. What *is* produced and sustained is the illusion of helplessness, an attitude of fatalism, and a bit of magical thinking. "We're too few, too tired, too old, too short on budget" — helplessness. "What is, is. Therefore nothing we do can change it" — fatalism. "Everything would be so great (read that as *easier*) if we just had Wednesday nights and dedicated parents again" — magical thinking.

So long as we point fingers at the kids and insist they shouldn't be this way . . . so long as we bemoan what the culture has now that we, the church, once had . . . so long as we blame the parents . . . we will be incapable of reaching the children and the youth and the parents at the very places in their lives where they have their deepest needs. Unless we are willing to say, "Whatever may have worked before probably won't work now," and "whatever we may have known before is not what we need to know now," we might as well sign the church up for hospice.

How Did It Come to This?

In his book *The Power of God at Home. Nurturing Our Children in Love and Grace*, J. Bradley Wigger points out:

> . . . when it comes to parents, many congregations are stuck in a vicious cycle. The more we expect congregations to handle spiritual nurture, the less parents see themselves as religious teachers or their homes as spiritual territory and, in turn, the more we expect of congregations. . . . Meanwhile, home gets left in the spiritual dust, a ghost town for faith. This only intensifies parents' own sense of inadequacy. Tragically, children, in turn, learn what they live — a sense of spiritual inferiority.[1]

Besides the dynamic of parents looking to congregations for the spiritual nurture of their children, there is the tendency of congregations themselves to equate "faith" and "faithful" with being present and active at church. In this model those parents who regularly attend worship and church school, serve as teachers, committee and board members, volunteer for Vacation Bible School, attend the fellowship events, help with fundraising, and generally stay involved in the life and work of the congregation are regarded as faithful and faith-filled. Those parents who are absent or only minimally involved are regarded as less faithful and, by association, less faith-filled. It's a short hop from these judgments to ones couched in terms of parents who are irresponsible, uncaring, and self-absorbed. The irony of the model that equates present-and-active with "faithful" and absent-and-inactive with "unfaithful" is that both parents and congregations are assuming that children's core faith formation will occur *in the congregation*. Meanwhile, the congregation assumes that (1) the present-and-active parents are actively reinforcing and building upon the efforts of the local church's education, mission-and-service, and worship ministries, and (2) the absent-and-uninvolved parents are the "problem" (whatever the problem may be).

What's wrong with this picture? Take a moment to reread the paragraph above and list, or highlight right here in the book, the assumptions at work. I'm serious. Do that before you go on. You'll need the list again in a few pages; it's a long one.

A second related dynamic at work here has to do with what I will call the geography of faith formation, families, and congregations. Since at least the Sunday School Movement of the 1800's in the United States, Protestant Christianity has narrowed the concept of church from the Body of Christ and the church universal to the local church explicitly existing at a specific geographical location and building. The *place* of church and the ministries and activities occurring *at that place* became paramount. Over the decades, and now centuries, we've made the place of church central, critical, even essential to our understanding of who we are as Christians and from where we "do" our Christianity. In the process, because the place was so important, we've assumed that sacred time would be there — would be made there and occur there — and we would come there, to that geographical place, for that sacred time. Ironically again, as our faith geography shifted from a home-plus-church culture to a church-place culture, what was lost was sacred time.

Sunday slipped from being true Sabbath — that day of worship and rest and renewal and joy set apart for families to step out of the world's time schedule, demands of productivity, and forced inequities. In its place, Sunday became the projects of church school, congregational meetings, youth fellowship, and special events. The transformations evolved gradually and innocently. No one within the church set out to rob the Sabbath of its holy and holistic restorative hours of grace. But it happened, right along with the transformations of the mainstream culture. So, here we are.

I'll pick up the topic of Sabbath, families, and the church briefly later in the chapter. Right now I want us to return to those grievances so often leveled at parents and children in particular, and the church and culture in general. By way of transition, here's a family story.

When our sons were young we fell into a little birthday-related routine that went like this.

Son: Mom, know what?
Mom: What?
Son: Next week's my birthday.
Mom: I know. That's so cool!
Son: And I'm turning 9.
Mom: Nine?!
Son (grinning): Yep, nine!
Mom (a little desperate): You can't turn nine. I just figured out eight!

These interchanges sent the boys into peals of laughter. I suspect they got enormous joy from the fact that their birthdays would come turning them a year older, and ready or not there was nothing their mom could do about it.

The church's experience hasn't been nearly as delightful or charming. Ready or not, here is the culture of today. Ready or not, here are the technologies (downloads, uploads, iPods, podcasts) and the communication styles (I just figured out call-waiting and I'm suppose to learn texting?). Ready or not, here is the post-modern clock — work more, do more, spend more, all without ceasing. Ready or not, here are the parents and the children who walk through our doors. There are the parents and children who have left. Out there are the parents and children who haven't given us a thought. No wonder many of us in the church look at each other and plead, "You can't turn into today. I just figured out yesterday."

Point-in-Time Exercise:
A Spoonful of Grieving Makes the Moving-On Go Down

- Step 1: List the grievances you are holding against "the parents," against the "children and the youth," against "the schools," and "the culture." If you have trouble getting started, look back to examples discussed earlier in the chapter. The list should be as long as it needs to be for you.

  Note: If you personally have already worked diligently to move past your own grievances, then use this list to identify those you have actually heard from others of the congregation as well as those you assume others have. In this case change the statement to "their grievance is that . . ." Be sure to tag each statement with "H" (heard) or "A" (assume) for reference. A worksheet for this activity can be found on www.thepilgrimpress.com.

- Step 2: Look back at your list of grievances. At the core of each one is loss and a sense of grief. I know, sometimes it's easier to focus on the displeasure or even anger you feel in connection with the grievance. Nonetheless, loss and grief are imbedded as well. So, put a name to each loss. What is gone that was once present? How long have you been feeling this loss? Add your answers to the statements you already listed as grievances.

- Step 3: Taking one grievance/loss at a time, reflect on these questions:
  - How will I put closure on this grief?
  - Who will I ask to hold me accountable to moving on?
  - How will I know I've let go?

  Now, for each grievance/loss, fill in the rest of this sentence: "My action will be . . ."

  Note: If you completed the list of grievances based on what you've heard and assumed, fill out the action list with specific ways of addressing the grievance statements and their underlying issues, either in a planned workshop format within the congregation's setting or as they surface within the work and planning sessions of the various ministries of your local church.

Having a Heart for Parents: Grinch-sized or God-sized?

I love the Dr. Seuss book, *How the Grinch Stole Christmas*. I love the rhymes, I love the whimsical drawings, I love Max with the oversized antlers tied to his head. I've known real people with the Grinch's wickedly conniving expression. I can't say that I love it on real people, but it so fits the Grinch. I love the feast of roast beast, I love little Sally Who's innocence and trust, I love the child-like awe that overtakes the Grinch when he realizes Christmas can't be bought or stolen. Most of all I love the Grinch's two-sizes-too-small heart that grows three sizes that Christmas dawn, and the goofy yet strangely endearing expression that spreads across his face.[2]

There is much that we in the local churches can't change immediately about the culture or about our communities. But we can work on ourselves — individually and as a group within the body of Christ. One of the places to start is putting together a profile of our attitudes and assumptions about parents that will help us look inside ourselves to ascertain if our hearts for parents are as God-sized as we think or actually more Grinch-sized.

You may remember that when we first meet the Grinch in Dr. Seuss's story, his consternation over the Whos' fuss and festivities of Christmas has almost the tone of righteous indignation. He's absolutely certain about the what and why of their activities and has not one good word to say nor one good thought to think about them. He hatches his plan to steal Christmas based on assumptions he's made about the meaning behind all the Whos' doings. If my conversations with local churches and readings in current church leadership and faith formation materials are any indication, we are operating with much the same certainty, based on assumptions and misread signals, about parents. In the process, our hearts for parents have constricted, like the Grinch's, to two sizes too small. It's time to reverse that process. Vital congregations strive for God-size hearts for parents.

Point-in-Time Exercise: Grinch-size Hearts to God-size Hearts

■ For this exercise you will need the assumptions you listed or highlighted earlier in this chapter and your completed grievance form from the previous Point-in-Time Exercise.

The goal here is to articulate or name those things that contribute to your congregation's constricted hearts for parents and then imagine ways for your congregation's heart to swell from Grinch-size to God-size for these parents. Remember, vital congregations strive for God-size hearts for parents.

▉ Step 1: Review the assumptions and grievances you've already identified. These give you clues for how, when it comes to parents, the congregation's heart is as Dr. Seuss said of the Grinch, "two sizes too small."[3] In some cases you may find whole insights not just clues. Write down your findings under the heading "When It Comes to Parents . . ."

▉ Step 2: Look at your "two sizes too small" list. I want you to think about three groups of parents, all related to your local church. *Caution:* Your task is not to name names and haggle over who fits each group, but to think about the groups as groups.

1. Those within the congregation — either as members or friends — who are "regulars." You define what "regular" means in your context.
2. Those who are not regulars but participate in some way(s) at some time(s). Again, you define this.
3. Those within the congregation who have children or youth but are, for all intents and purposes, here in name only. For example, a couple may have been regular attendees before their baby was born but now are rarely present. Or a parent may have been confirmed in the church during her or his youth but hasn't been active since.

▉ With these three groups in mind plus the metaphor of the Grinch's heart that was two sizes too small, use the following questions to strategize:

• What can you — individually or as a group — actually change in the next week that would affect a growth in your heart-size for parents? What about in the next few months? By next year?
• What do you need in order to make that growth of heart?
• Where is Jesus in this growth-of-heart-size process?
• How is your faith challenged and blessed by this growth of heart size?
• How is your congregation's mission furthered?
Put your ideas in a list labeled "Growing God-sized Hearts for Parents."

Pause in the Point-in-Time Exercise

Now, when the defense is made that the church already has a God-size heart for parents — after all, we do this and that, and they have this and that, and they could have this and that, and so forth — then what?

Good question. In fact, it's an important question. Often we lose sight of why we set out in a particular direction, like we can lose sight of the forest for the trees. So first, let's remind ourselves that the destination of this chapter is the equipping of ourselves (we are the "et al." in the "Parents et al." of the chapter title) to equip and support twenty-first century parents in home-based faith formation. Second, let us be frank about our current situation. If parents felt equipped for faith formation and had established faith practices that were enriching the spiritual lives and faith of their children, we would most likely know about it in the congregation because it would be evident. It would be evident in the talk and questions, discussion and priorities, joys and passions of the parents and the children around faith and faith-filled living. Third, I suspect you are reading this chapter because you are looking for something: paths that lead toward re-establishing homes of faith and formation, affirmation that conclusions you've drawn are on the right track, ways to help others see the need for a change in direction. Any or all of these require exploration and follow-through on your part. I'm offering avenues and tools for the necessary exploration and work.

Identifying in what ways you or your local congregation evidence God-size hearts for parents is completely appropriate as part of the "Grinch-size Hearts to God-size Hearts" Point-in-Time exercise — *so long as that is not where you linger and stall, or where you let your congregation linger and stall.* We in the church are very good at two things when it comes to protecting ourselves. We swath ourselves in layers of bubble wrap filled with righteous reiterations of all the "but we do's." Then with a sleight of hand we swap those righteous reiterations of all the "but we do's" into the space where we would otherwise have to pick up the challenge and dig into unfamiliar or even yet-to-be-imagined ministries and methods. Beware the bubble wrap and the sleight of hand!

Point-in-Time Exercise Continued

■ Step 3: Take it to the next level. Vital congregations think and act, feel and respond in terms of ministries. Those ministries are informed by the life and work — the ministries — of Jesus and are energized by the Holy

Spirit. Therefore vital congregations will not only seek to swell their hearts from Grinch-sized to God-sized for parents already tied to the church. They will also seek to swell their hearts for parents who are not already within the circle of the congregation's arms.

When it comes to parents who have yet to give us a thought — parents who are un-churched themselves, are disillusioned about church and Christianity, or are wounded from previous encounters with organized religion — how is the congregation's heart two sizes too small? Use your notes from Step 1. With these yet-to-be-met parents in mind plus the metaphor of the Grinch's heart that was two sizes too small, strategize using the following questions:

- What can you — individually or as a group — actually change in the next week that would affect a growth in your heart-size for these parents? What about in the next few months? By next year?
- What do you need in order to make that growth of heart?
- Where is Jesus in this growth-of-heart-size process?
- How is your faith challenged and blessed by this growth of heart size?
- How is your congregation's mission furthered?

Put your ideas in a list labeled "Growing God-sized Hearts for Parents Who Have Yet to Think of Us."

▨ Step 4: Stop and reflect. What have you learned about yourself and/ or your congregation through the process of this Point-in-Time Exercise? What perspective(s) have you gained that you did not have before? What insights do you have now relative to ministering to and with parents so that they may minister to and with their children and youth? What do you want to do next? What do you need next?

Write down your reflections. I know I've said this and written this before and, yes, I'm saying it and writing it again. Don't just think your responses. Put them into writing. Don't worry about polishing them. No one's going to grade them. The process of writing brings truths and insights into being in a way that only thinking about things does not. Don't let that richness get lost.

Away with Assumptions: Listening to Parents

If you've done the point-in-time exercises in this chapter so far you have insights into not only your personal assumptions and behaviors relative to parents but also the resident assumptions and behaviors of your church. Now comes the time to seek information and potential direction from the parents themselves. There will be at least four groups of parents who can give you what you need:

1. Those within the congregation — either as members or friends — who are "regulars."

2. Those who are not regulars but participate in some way(s) at some time(s).

3. Those within the congregation who have children or youth but are for all intents and purposes, here in name only.

4. Those who are not already within the circle of the congregation's arms — those un-churched, those disillusioned about church and Christianity, or those wounded from previous encounters with organized religion.

Notice the four groups are the same as those identified in the previous point-in-time exercise.

"How shall we go about obtaining the information we need from all these groups of parents?" you ask. Well, there will be talking involved and note-taking as well, but probably not the way you're thinking at the moment. We do a lot of talking in our local churches, much of it associated with the business and organizational aspects of life as a congregation with a building and grounds and programs. As you've already discovered through the point-in-time exercises, we also do too much assuming and reiterating of those assumptions. We don't do much active listening. Pastors, Christian education professionals, parish nurses, Stephens Ministers and youth leaders probably do the yeoman's share of active listening as they attend to individuals, families, and sometimes small groups in crisis. The rest of the time, even these trained church leaders usually go into task-specific or problem-solving modes of talking and listening.

The other tack we take when we are looking for information is the ubiquitous survey. Numerous churches put a Time and Talent sheet into the annual fund drive and stewardship materials. Christian education committees send out surveys to adults in hope of discovering topics they want to explore and would actually attend during the next program year. Church School teachers complete surveys on curriculum resources they sample and use. Youth leaders send out parent surveys and youth surveys to help determine directions in programming. Surveys are sent through the mail, completed during meetings, folded into worship bulletins so as to be completed and placed in the offering baskets. Responses are tallied. Decisions are made and, in some form, announced to those affected. It's a fairly painless approach, though how accurate a guideline any survey provides is up for debate, especially if the goal is to get input from "everyone" but only the conscientious, the active, or the axe-grinders return the completed survey.

Joining together with parents to help re-establish homes of faith and formation is too essential to trust to surveys. This will take authentic commitment to active listening, forming and asking core questions, respectful follow-up questions, earnest requests to "say some more about that," and genuine desire to learn from the parents themselves.

When was the last time you gathered a group of parents together and listened pastorally to them? I don't mean setting up appointments to go over baptism details, recruiting them for some task, or making hospital calls. I mean creating spaces and unhurried time to really listen to them in their roles as parents. Leading them into conversation with prompts such as:

"Tell me about your greatest joys at the moment."

"What are you learning about yourselves as parents?"

"How is the community helping you parent? How is the community a stressor for your family?"

"Please talk to me about those issues or situations that worry you. Where do you find the support you need? Where do you find comfort? What gives you strength? What ways are you finding to feed your spiritual self? What ways are you finding to support and nurture your children's spiritual selves?"

"Talk to me about what our church is providing that's helpful to you and your children's faith. What are we missing? What are we not seeing? What could be of more help? In what ways would that help?"

Think of Bill Moyers' interview style and you'll capture the texture and tone of the conversations I'm suggesting.

Several years ago I put together a brief think piece to capture some of what I was hearing from church leaders about parents and from parents themselves. The particular issue was about parents and children not being present in the church building on Sunday mornings "like they used to be." In this case, "like they used to be" referred to earlier eras during which the congregation had experienced significantly higher attendance numbers. I'm sliding that piece into this chapter now as an example of some ruminating and insights that deep listening to parents can stimulate.

Think Piece: Cultural Rifts in the Faith-Time Continuum

Parents are saying, "Sunday is the only morning (day) we have together…

> … to sleep in
> … to eat together
> … to have a relaxing morning
> OR
> … to do the shopping
> … laundry
> … yard work

Parents are taking Sabbath … but without knowing the spiritual dynamics of it and without the blessing of the church. The church, though, keeps saying (and expecting), "You should be at church."

What are we — the church — doing to help parents carve out worship and educational space and still have the down time they and the kids so desperately need?

We need a new paradigm for twenty-first century Sabbath and twenty-first century worship/education. We must not just keep saying, "Parents shouldn't allow their kids to be in so many activities," or "Families should be in church and Sunday School," or "Well, sports has taken over everything," or "This faith formation should be happening in the family home."

We must be the ones to rethink, recreate, re-imagine, and then model (remodel) a faith-full life in a society that takes no notice of Sunday as anything more than part of the weekend. I have become convinced that we need to re-conceptualize the whole of Sabbath and Sunday, including what we think needs to happen in "Sunday School."

Culturally speaking…

- No child or youth needs more hours in school.
- Each child and youth needs safe and uncluttered "space" — a giant rest-space like in a musical score or a "comma" so they can take a breath in their weeks and in their days.
- Each parent needs a safe and uncluttered "space" too.

But along with that, each needs core group(s) where they wrestle with the toxicity of the culture and begin to discover the restorative nature of the gospel.

If parents can't find the "good news" of the gospel in the structures and assumptions of the church as it is, then either:

1. we don't really know the "good news" and its relevance to the culture-stricken . . . we just assume that we do . . .
     OR
2. we've sung the same song so long we think everybody knows its meaning and worth because it has meaning and worth for us.

What are Jesus' "good news" words by which we can choose to live in counterpoint with the culture?

What are Jesus' "good news" words by which we can offer balm, encouragement, sustenance, and new life to parents in a toxic culture, and by which they will be able to lead their children to life-giving options as well?

Groans and Moans

Should I duck and run for cover about now? Here I am suggesting that the church leadership and other interested parties invest precious time gathering parents and having heart-to-heart conversations with them a la Bill Moyers, when the leadership itself is feeling as stretched for time as are the parents. I imagine some of you are thinking, "Only a professor with time on her hands could think up something like this and suggest it to those in the 'real local church world'."

Not so. First of all, this professor rarely has time on her hands. If you have some to share, I'd be glad to have it. Second, while I've been a professor for over a decade, I've been a pastor and teacher all my adult life. Third, I did an active listening process as recently as six months before the time of this writing. It had to do with educational programming for adults in the local church I attend. After conversations with the minister and Director of Christian Education, I volunteered to meet with those longing for a type of faith-dialogue group that didn't yet exist. No surveys, no assumptions, lots of thoughtful questions, gentle probing, genuine care for the faith lives of those involved, and active listening. A new ministry emerged from what was shared, one that continues because those participating find it so spiritually nurturing and sustaining.

I've learned over the years the power of active, authentic listening and genuine interest when it comes to discovering the faith hungers and desires of those I serve in the local and wider church and then converting what I've heard into ministries that actually feed and sustain individuals' spiritual lives. Pastors understand how critical active listening is in pastoral care situations. It is just as vital in the realm of educational and faith formation ministries. In fact, when pastoral care ears and eyes are used in the arenas of faith formation and education, authentic ministries develop that would otherwise not. This is not about breaching confidentiality. This is about taking our cues from the very people with whom we seek to provide ministry, including the ministry of faith formation.

Stories from the Field: The Power of Storybooks
When Read Aloud for Parents

I'm taking the long way around to get to the ministry hinted at in the title of this section, but please bear with me. I think you'll find the end point worth the trip.

When our children were young, the local public library had summer bedtime story hour for parents and young children. The boys and I went every week. Children could come in their pajamas and slippers so that once they returned home they could climb right into bed. We lived around the corner from the library, so for us it was extra fun. We walked or I pulled the boys in our wooden wagon.

During those same years a young mother who was a member of our church did some childcare for our boys. Her role in a local parenting co-op was to read and review children's picture story books, making recommendations about which were the best ones for children's nurture and growth. She loaned me two enormous boxes of the books she'd reviewed and recommended and I spent one of the most wonderful weeks between Christmas and New Year's reading aloud to our boys several times a day, then reading to myself during their afternoon rest times. Let's just say that their personal libraries reflect a good deal of what we read together.

Also during those years I worked with an amazing Christian educator, Virginia Less, whose passion was resourcing the teachers, families, and children of the congregation. Her title as a Commissioned Minister of the United Church of Christ was Library Resource Coordinator, and her ministry touched the lives of congregations across the greater Chicago metropolitan area and surrounding counties. Fortunately for me, she lived out that same passion within our congregation. We had a marvelous church library filled with resources for the pastors and laity, adults, youth, and children. Over a period of several years she and I worked together to select and purchase children's picture story books that both explicitly and implicitly nurtured the faith and spiritual lives of the congregation's children. The books in the church library were meant to be borrowed, and borrowed they were! Then in the late fall, when Virginia and the Christian education committee provided an on-site book sale for the congregation, these faith-supportive children's books were part of it, as a service to parents wanting quality story books for their young ones.

I warned you I was taking the long way around, but we're almost there. In my role as one of the ministers of the congregation, I worked with the children and their parents regularly. I heard their tales of child-rearing and was asked myriad questions about how to talk with their children about the death of a grandparent, loss of a pet, illness of a parent, being kind to others while remaining safe, where God lives, why Jesus died, and what the little bread cubes are on those plates in church. They also asked about what they could buy or give their children that was "Christian."

I tested an idea out with several of the parents of young children: Would it be helpful to have an evening exploring good picture story books for children to discover how they could be used to help the parents convey important Christian beliefs and values? "Yes, absolutely," came back the replies. That's what we did. I set up one of the carpeted church school rooms so that adults could sit on the floor or in rocking chairs. The church's collection of wonderful picture story books plus others from my boys' book shelves were set out invitingly on a cloth-covered six-foot-long table. For two hours we "played" in the books, reading them aloud to one another. I remember getting to a point in one I was reading that was a tender spot. I teared up and had to stop for a minute. Others had also teared up. One mom said, "I couldn't read that to my kids. I'd be crying like you are." I passed around the tissue and replied, "Read it anyway, and cry at the tender places. It'll give you a wonderful opportunity to share your feelings with your children, give them words to put with those feelings, and to ask them how they're feeling about what's happening in the story. It will also give you a moment to let them know that God feels what we're feeling, loves us, and will help us through our sad times."

That single evening of read-aloud stories with parents set the stage for further ministries with them and their children. More than that, it gave them a model for establishing a faith-formative practice in their homes that could continue as their children grew. It provided hands-on experience with the many excellent books available and hearts-on experience with some of the stories. A number of the families cultivated a pattern of reading aloud clear into the middle school years, when the children tackled reading chapters aloud from books like the *Chronicles of Narnia* and various series written by Madeleine L'Engle. In these instances, the discussions around faith and what it means to believe, to depend on a loving God, and to live a Christ-like life became richer and richer for the young persons and the adults.

My colleague, Rev. Leah Matthews, once said of home visits with mothers of little ones, "It's amazing the good theology you can get into while playing on the floor with a toddler and mom." From my evening with storybooks and parents I add, "It's amazing the good theology you can get into while reading children's books aloud with parents."

Equipping Ourselves, Equipping Parents:
The Gospel's Restorative Power

I suggested earlier, particularly in the think piece "Cultural Rifts in the Faith-Time Continuum," that we must identify the Good News Jesus brings to parents and to their children, and make that Good News accessible and understandable to families of every configuration in this twenty-first century culture. So far, I've not come across an individual book that spells out what we need in simple straight forward ABCs. While such a book sounds on the surface like a good idea, I'm not so sure it is. I say this because if someone else has done the hard work for us, we have little ownership of the suggestions. Worse, we have not struggled with our scriptures or the theology and faith-language that rolls off our tongues, flies from our fingers, and shows up in our bulletins to the point of being able to clarify what we're talking about and to what we are alluding. Christianity, like all religions, has a language and lexicon all its own. Most of us forget how to speak plainly of the truths behind the vocabulary of our faith. Leaders of vital congregations must be able to not only speak the language of Christian faith but also be able to translate it for those new to it. Sort of like Christianity as a second language.

Back to focusing on the gospel's restorative power for parents and families. In his book *The Power of God at Home. Nurturing Our Children in Love and Grace*, J. Bradley Wigger suggests that one thread running through the scriptures is place-displacement-home.[4] Using this thread, he leads the reader through the biblical narrative from creation in Genesis to the new creation in the risen Christ and envisioned ultimately in Revelation. The reader discovers perhaps for the first time the ups and downs, the hope-hopelessness-renewed hope experienced by the people of God across time and geography. The reader sees and feels the undulations of the biblical narrative that capture first the sense of place, then the trauma of displacement, then the joy of home repeatedly.

In terms of the gospel and its restorative power for parents and families, I see real potential in the points of reference Wigger offers. For example, he suggests that, just as the Temple in Jerusalem had served as God's dwelling among God's people for generations, Jesus embodied God's dwelling among his followers. This is "place." It is "where" Jesus' ministry brought hope. The crucifixion suddenly displaced the hope that Jesus' life and teachings had created. I am reminded of the little poem that asks, "Where shall I go, what shall I do/You without me, I without you?" Only this time it's Jesus' followers asking, "Where shall we go, what shall we do?" and "Who are we without our Rabbi and Messiah Jesus?" The answer comes with the resurrection. The resurrection brings us home. There is a new creation, there is new life, there is even a new community where we live and breathe and have our being. Jesus has gone home. We have found home. When we die we will go home.

Wigger concludes "The Story of Home" chapter with these thoughts:

> The Bible puts an understanding of family and of home in the largest imaginable perspective. The Bible puts the struggles and hopes of living — all those plots we live daily — in the largest imaginable perspective. Underneath it all is a conviction: God is at home among mortals. This conviction sets the stage for considering what it might mean for God to be at home in our own particular lives, for God to be at home in the lives of our children.[5]

Another restorative theme and teaching in the gospels is the good news of abundant life. In a culture that too often equates "abundant" with affluence and material abundance, we have much to gain from the refreshment offered by Jesus' teachings of abundant life. Here we can draw on the Quaker and Mennonite traditions and practices of simplicity and simple living to help us reorient our quests for what will fill and fulfill our deepest hungers. I'm grateful to Michael Schut for editing *Simpler Living, Compassionate Life: A Christian Perspective*, which contains a collection of rich essays from faithful practitioners of simpler living as well as study guides for groups and individuals. Another book I'm finding helpful is Janet Luhrs' *The Simple Living Guide: A Sourcebook for Less Stressful, More Joyful Living.*[6]

A related theme and teaching would be Jesus' focus on the common good in contrast to one's own interests. I've found my thinking stimulated by Laurent Parks Daloz and his colleagues' work discussed in *Common Fire: Leading Lives of Commitment in a Complex World* as well as Anne Colby's and William Damon's *Some Do Care*. Dale Rosenberger puts feet to vision in *Outreach and Mission for Vital Congregations.*[7]

The restorative power of Sabbath, touched on in the think piece "Cultural Rifts in the Faith-Time Continuum," is another source of good news. Authors who I've found helpful include Donna Schaper, Dorothy Bass, J. Bradley Wigger, Wayne Muller, Christopher D. Ringwald and Tilden Edwards. The list of Recommended Resources at the back of this book offers titles and publication information.

Forgiveness and grace hold a priority place in the gospel's restorative power. I can think of few groups more in need of deeply experienced forgiveness and grace than those in the role of parent. Helping parents discover how to offer that experience to their children and to one another will occur best as they encounter stories of God's forgiveness and grace in the lives of others and begin to recognize moments of God's forgiveness and grace in their own lives. Naming their own experiences will also help parents help their children recognize God's activity in their young lives.

As the Israelites experienced God in the midst of parenting and families, so also do Christians. The New Testament narratives reveal Jesus restoring life to families and taking parents seriously. He interprets his own identity within the relationship of divine parent and child. Vital congregations will take parents and families seriously as well, searching and discovering how the church can nurture and sustain the faith formation of parents so that together the congregation and the parents will nurture and sustain the children and youth in their faith formation.

Equipping Ourselves, Equipping Parents: Getting in Gear

Rarely, maybe never, can a program or ministry of one setting be exactly duplicated in another setting and be meaningful. Contexts and congregations vary. Having said that, below you will find concrete ideas for cultivating a congregational environment and attitude that is authentic in its desire to help parents just coming through the church doors and those already inside, those who are new to church, those who are new to Christianity, and all other interested parties re-establish homes of faith and formation. Two of them include details. Have fun filling in your own details with the others! Realize that your ministries will change in response to the needs expressed by parents — needs that you will hear through your active, authentic listening and genuine interest. Try not to fear the reality of necessary changes and alterations. Trust in God's love and invigorating Spirit to empower your ministries.

Greeting the Children

The children's finger rhyme says, "Here's the church and here's the steeple. Open the doors and see all the people." When you greet one another in the church hallways who do you "see" as part of your greeting? The adults? The children with the adults? Who do you actually greet, shake hands with, smile directly at, chat with for a few moments?

Try directing your greetings to the children first, then moving on to the grown-ups. "Good morning, Lyndsi and Jake." "Good to see you, Hazel." Oh, and be sure to include all the children in a family, especially if, for example, lots of attention is otherwise being showered on one in particular such as a new baby. I know it's the complete opposite of traditional etiquette. What we're working toward is more intentional inclusion of all the members of the family group in the greeting. For all kinds of reasons — not the least of which may be the effort put into getting themselves and the children dressed, fed, and here on time — acknowledging the youngsters in their own right can go a long way to helping parents feel welcomed and cared for by the congregation. Besides that, we really are remiss if we don't work to learn the names and the faces of all the members of our particular part of the body of Christ.

One of my favorite greetings, especially if I do not know the youngsters' names, is a "Good morning, young woman" or "Good morning, young man" delivered close to their eye level. I watch their reactions and take my cues from them, responding respectfully whether they are shy or eager to talk. Then I greet the adult(s) with them. Try directing your goodbyes to those with children in a similar way.

Advent and Christmas as Models

No matter what else occurs in the life of a congregation during the year, it's safe to say Christmas will receive some added attention. If your tradition observes Advent, then special liturgical attention will also be given to the four weeks preceding Christmas. If your congregation is in the know about the twelve days of Christmas and the celebration of Epiphany you have even more grounding in the "reason for the season."

Now imagine that almost everyone coming to worship in the weeks leading up to Christmas does *not* know even the basics of the Christ Child's birth, let alone all the details. Is this a pastor's worst nightmare, or the best Advent and Christmas ever? Better to move forward with the assumption that there are indeed those coming through the door who know only the secular versions of Christmas — Santa, Rudolph the Red-Nosed Reindeer, Frosty the Snowman and company, Jingle Bells, Here Comes Santa Claus, and the Twelve Days of Christmas. Bah, Humbug!

Use what you have and package it for carry-out!

- Do you light candles in an Advent wreath? Send Advent wreaths, complete with candles, home with everyone. Be sure to include background information on why a wreath, why candles, why four weeks, why the specific color(s) of the candles, and how the tradition got started.
- Do you sing Advent and Christmas hymns? Send home a CD of the choir, one talented musical family, or the congregation's own voices singing the hymns. Be sure to include copies of the words. And yes, stay inside the copyright laws!
- Do you read scripture during worship? Put together a booklet of the birth narratives of Matthew and Luke. Print them in parallel columns so everyone can compare the two accounts. Include the opening chapter of John's gospel and also the gospel of Mark. Add a few search-and-find type questions such as who wrote about the shepherds and when do the magi finally arrive. Then post Frequently Asked Questions about Christmas, along with the answers, on the church's website.
- Do you have a Christmas pageant or a retelling of the Nativity through drama? Arrange for pictures to be taken during a costumed rehearsal. Add captions to them describing what's going on. Do not name the children and

adults, only the characters. Make multiple copies of the photos available on the day of the pageant or Nativity reenactment so that worshippers of all ages can watch for particular scenes and can retell the story at home or on their own using the photos.

- Assemble Christmas gift bags for parents and get them into parents' hands early in the season. It's important for congregations to "gift" the parents of young children with starter materials for home-based faith formation as part of their ministry. Staci Williams, local Christian Educator and Lay Minister in the Brethren Church, suggests that "Christmas provides a wonderful teaching opportunity that parents can sometimes overlook. The church can help shift children's attention from Santa Claus to Jesus by providing families of young children with a Christmas gift bag."[8] She describes a gift bag that includes items that can be easily used every day. Put in a children's book of the Christmas story that stays close to the biblical account of Jesus' birth. Add cookie cutters in the shape of important people and things from the story such as a baby in a manger, an angel, the shepherds, a candle, a star, a man and a woman to represent Joseph and Mary. Also include simple materials and directions for a make-at-home nativity set.[9]

What works at Christmas can be adapted to other church seasons and other biblical narratives. The reason children and adults who have "always" been in church know the Christmas narratives so intimately is because they've participated in those narrative all their church lives. Imagine the degree of intimacy children and parents would have with Lent and Easter, with Pentecost and Common Time, with social justice, compassion for the needy, and biblical stewardship if we helped them experience and learn of these both within the church building and within their homes. Use Christmas and Advent as models for year-long faith formation.

Invest in Bibles and other good books for the children and families.
- Put out a display of books so parents and children can pick them up and look through them.
- Invest in Bibles for various ages and use them everywhere, not just in church school, and give copies to families as well as individual children.
- Host a book fair for the congregation so that children can show parents which books interest them, and parents can select faith-formative gifts for their families.

Focus on C.S. Lewis' Chronicles of Narnia.
- Make use of the film version of *The Lion, the Witch, and the Wardrobe* as a resource to pull families together to explore themes of good and evil, betrayal and forgiveness, faith and sacrifice.
- Provide viewing guides — be brave and create your own if need be — that help draw children, youth, and parents' attention to key Christian themes and theology.
- Look at what's happening in the narrative through Lucy's eyes, as she's the youngest of the four children.
- Consider using *The Lion, the Witch, and the Wardrobe* as a Lenten study designed for use across the ages, and encourage your congregation to participate across the generations. The walls of your building could become a giant story-board incorporating images from the book and film with scripture passages of God's presence, Jesus' suffering, death and resurrection, and the disciples' responses before and after Jesus passion.
- Host a "Return from Narnia" event to mark the end of the experience if you've invited families to participate during a particular season or set of weeks.

Create a church-family blog for exploring Christian themes in the children's and youth's books. Remember the Learning Cone from Chapter 2.
- While you may know little or nothing about setting up or using a blog, a congregation member may make use of them frequently and may be willing to take on this particular ministry.
- This blog could be for "parents" only, not children.
- Have a short orientation session with parents interested in using the blog as a resource and launch it as a ministry of the church.
- Every so often, ask the blog host to compile a publishable update of the information generated in the blog and post that on the church's website or make hardcopies to distribute to current and visiting parents.

Be Brave!

At the end of this book you will find a list of wonderful resources — okay, they're books — full of ideas and examples of ways local congregations can intentionally create a pro-parent/pro-family culture that can help anchor parents and children in an otherwise whirlwind and toxic culture. Remember, the temptation is to rummage through the pages, grab ideas, and slap them onto whatever is already happening or not happening in your setting and expect great miracles to result. Don't do that! Use some of the processes you've encountered throughout this chapter as guides for discerning and deciding. Borrow copies of various books and create an in-house/in-church book club. See what discussions and formative moments come out of a book club environment that wouldn't have surfaced in a monthly Christian education committee meeting.

The wonderful gentleman who was at one time my college choir director, then the Academic Dean when I came to Defiance College, is also the choir director of our church. When he gathers some of us as Christmas carolers to sing at various public venues plus the college president's large open-house, there is always one song the rest of us worry about messing up. We make worried faces when he tells us it is next. But he looks confidently at us and softly says, "Be brave."

You don't have to know how successful you will be when you begin a ministry. You don't have to have all the figurative notes down perfectly to make music and enrich those with whom you minister or to whom you want your ministry to reach. Do your homework. Gather those with willingness. Stoke the flickers or embers of passion. Remember Whose you are and Who you serve. Most of all, "Be brave."

Four

Congregational Biblical (II)literacy: An Elephant in the Room and The Cost of Pastors' "Secret Knowledge"

> Your word is a lamp to my feet and a light to my path.
> (Psalm 119:105.)

> No one after lighting a lamp puts it under a bushel basket, but on a lamp stand, and it gives light to all in the house.
> (Matthew 5:15.)

Naming the Elephant in the Room

All right, let's just say it. Most of the people in our local churches are biblically illiterate.

Most cannot name all the books of the Bible, do not recognize which books belong to the New Testament and which to the "Old Testament," i.e., the Hebrew Bible. They do not know that the books of the Bible are not organized in a systematically chronological order or that the books themselves differ widely in authorship, genre, time period and purpose. They do not know there are two creation stories, or that there are two narratives about how many animals Noah loaded into the ark — one saying two each, a male and a female, the other saying seven of each kind. Our people do not know the major narratives of the patriarchs enough so that sermons, film studies, book discussions of novels could allude to them or use them as comparisons and the people would "get" the connection.

Most congregants know of the Ten Commandments and Moses and the Exodus through exposure to Cecil B. DeMille's movie *The Ten Commandments* and DreamWorks' animated version, *Prince of Egypt*. Few could actually list the Ten Commandments, even out of order. Most of the people in the pew think the prophets foretold the future even into the twenty-first century, not that they spoke truth to power and called the people into accountability for creating and maintaining a socio-economic culture that disregarded the needs of the many to protect and enhance the wealth and privilege of the few. Most are unaware that the prophets did not all live at the same time, that they came from very different backgrounds, and that they weren't the only prophets around by any means. Most congregants have no understanding of the political and historical, let alone religious, reasons the Babylonian exile occurred or that Israel never truly recovered from that exile.

Setting aside the inter-testamentary period and its books and moving right along to the New Testament, most congregants do not know which books contain the narratives about Jesus, and that these therefore are the ones called gospels. Most would be surprised to discover that the entire Christmas story as it is played out by children in annual pageants is not in all four gospels, nor told in its entirety in any single gospel, that the magi did not arrive at the baby Jesus' birth but about two years later, that Mark's gospel has no birth narrative — it opens with Jesus' adult baptism — and nor does John's, which opens with "In the beginning was the Word" and then jumps to John the Baptist and Jesus as adults.

Most congregants have never compared Jesus' travels as recorded in the various gospels, either to locate them on an accurate map or to see if they differ across the gospels. The same could be said of never comparing the accounts of Holy Week either. Most congregants do not know that the gospel writers wrote their gospels many years after Jesus' resurrection, that the writers authored their gospels decades apart from each other, that each addressed and fashioned the message of his gospel to meet the needs of a particular early Christian community at a particularly critical point in time, and that the issues and audiences differed widely. Most congregations do not know that the gospels are not the oldest writings of the New Testament but that Paul's letters and even his death predate the writing of the gospels.

Okay, I'm going to stop there and not go into Paul and the other authors of epistles and writings, including Revelation. I know you've gotten the point. However, not to put too fine a point on the point . . . there are all those recurring biblical terms like manna and Baal and Canaanites and parable and Sadducee and Pharisee that are misunderstood or glossed over.

The Cost of Pastors' "Secret Knowledge"

There is a cost of pastors' secret knowledge. What secret knowledge?

Point-in-Time Exercise: What Secret Knowledge?

■ "No one after lighting a lamp puts it under the bushel basket, but on a lamp stand, and it gives light to all in the house." Matthew 5:15

In order to answer the question "What Secret Knowledge?" pastors and professional church educators need to recognize the sheer amount and type of knowledge about the Bible they possess that the general congregants do not. Hence, I have provided this point-in-time exercise.

■ Part One (everyone completes this): Put a check next to all that apply.

_____ Attended theological school/seminary

_____ Completed at least one course in biblical studies

_____ Completed a survey-type course on the Hebrew Bible

_____ Completed a survey-type course on the New Testament

_____ Completed one or more courses on specific Hebrew Bible topics books such as Pentateuch, the major prophets.

_____ Completed one or more courses on specific New Testament topics books such as the gospels, Paul's letters

_____ Completed one or more courses focusing on a single book of the Hebrew Bible

_____ Completed one or more courses focusing on a single book in the New Testament

_____ Completed one or more courses on the Hebrew language

_____ Completed one or more courses on the Greek language

(If you do this in a group, individuals could be invited, as they are able, to stand or raise their hands in response to the prompts. The visual component adds to the impact of the exercise.)

With Parts Two and Three comes the need for designating two groups based on experiences and roles. To help simplify directions and to avoid creating the illusion of first and second class participants, the following playful designations will be used:

- Robins: church professionals (e.g. clergy, church educators) and clergy spouses (I've been informed that clergy spouses who are laity, while not formally trained in seminary, often find a better fit within the clergy/church educator/seminary-trained category than the laity category)
- Bluebirds: Laity

▰ Part Two A. Questions specifically for the Robins. Bluebirds skip to Two B. Robins, put a check next to all that apply.

____You consider the congregation you serve to be biblically literate.
____Your congregational members are as knowledgeable as you are about scripture.

▰ Part Two B. Questions specifically for Bluebirds. Robins skip these questions, read the paragraph below, and then go on to Part Three A. Bluebirds, put a check next to all that apply.

____You consider the congregation of which you are a part to be biblically literate.
____You consider the congregational members to be as knowledgeable as your pastor and/or church educator are about scripture.
____You consider yourself to be biblically literate.

Robins and Bluebirds, look back over the checklists of Parts One and Two. Notice the disconnect? That's what I mean by pastors' — and seminary graduate professional church educators' — "secret knowledge." We have all this training in biblical studies. Some of us have been fortunate enough to have had eminent Biblical scholars as our professors, for goodness' sake. Yet the net result is that we have these lamps with this incredible light tucked safely away under all manner of baskets and that's where, except for a shimmer here or a glimmer there, the light stays. If we're going to address and eliminate biblical illiteracy we have to deal with this disconnect.

■ Part Three A, the next step for Robins. Bluebirds skip (okay, fly) to Part Three B. Robins, sort your lists from Parts One and Two by the following criteria:

- I've been able to teach/preach about this "in public"
- I haven't taught/preached about it "in public." By "in public" I mean from the pulpit during worship, within a Bible study, adult education class, confirmation class and so forth.

■ Now ask yourself the questions below. Write down your insights. If you are doing this exercise in a group of other clergy and church educators, pair with a colleague and discuss your discoveries.

- What dynamics were present when you were able to teach/preach about those topics you listed above?
- What dynamics were/are present that you haven't taught/preached about the other topics you listed above?

■ Part Three B, the next step for Bluebirds. Robins go on to Part Four. The Bluebirds will meet you there. Now, Bluebirds, refer to your lists from Parts One and Two and ask yourself the question below.

Write down your interests. "Everything" is not an acceptable answer, nor is "almost everything." Give yourself some specifics. If you are doing this exercise in a group, get together with one other lay person and compare your lists. Preferably pair up with someone whose ideas you think may be different than your own. Also, discuss any involvement you've had with the study of the Bible and/or your choices not to study the Bible.

- What do you wish you were learning about the Bible, the books of the Bible, and so forth?

■ Part Four, Robins and Bluebirds (i.e., everyone). What did you discover through your lists and discussions?

I will say it again. Pastors and seminary-graduate professional church educators have these lamps with this incredible light tucked safely away under all manner of baskets and that's where, except for a shimmer here or a glimmer there, it stays. If we're going to address and eliminate biblical illiteracy, we have to deal with this disconnect. If congregations are going to be vital we have to deal with this disconnect in order to reduce biblical illiteracy and foster knowledge, understanding, and exploration of scripture in its place.

Resistance — Futile or Fertile?

Anyone familiar with Star Trek's *Next Generation* television and movie series associates the word futile with the Borg's mission to assimilate all sentient beings into their collective, whether the other sentient beings wish to be assimilated or not. Every time the Borg show up, they announce repeatedly and in no uncertain terms, "Resistance is futile." Fortunately the Borg meet their match several times, as the crew of the Starship Enterprise proves that resistance is not futile but does require creativity, persistence, and sacrifices. In the universe of Star Trek, the Borg are the enemy to be resisted and defeated at all cost. Those who resist in any way possible are the heroes.

In our universe of the body of Christ and Christ's body manifested in the local church, one hopes — okay, I hope — that resistance to engaging Holy Scripture will be minimal. I'm not so naive as to imagine there won't be some, or that some resistance won't be ferocious. I have colleagues who have had to metaphorically gird up their loins and do battle with members of the congregation who declare in deed, and sometimes in actual word, that the pastor (seminary-trained in biblical study, no less) may be competent to preach, pray with the sick and dying, and conduct funerals but was not competent to lead them in Bible study. In these instances it was not a case of having well-equipped lay leadership stepping into a responsible faith formation leadership role. It was that these particular lay leaders wanted only their interpretation of scripture available to church and community members. Underlying that agenda was resistance rooted along the lines of, "I've made up my mind. Don't confuse me with the facts." At the other end of the spectrum I have colleagues who run into the proverbial brick wall as they attempt to integrate biblical study as part of the agenda of the church council, trustees, or diaconate meetings. "Pastor, we're not here for Bible study, we're here to do the business of the church. Just stick to an opening prayer."

What resistance will be awakened in individuals when an intentional Bible literacy intervention begins? What resistance will you meet as you create environments designed to bring people face to face with the results of biblical research, interpretation, and understandings that go way beyond the last Sunday school lesson they had as a child, youth, or even adult? You may be surprised. The open resistance originates from fear of losing one's faith, of having one's faith destroyed. "If such-and-such isn't historically factual and therefore true, then everything I've been taught and believe in must be false as well." "But my faith will collapse if you make me accept this new information." This fear is not always explicitly stated but is implicit behind the wall of challenges and strong emotions often expressed. Whether we think it's justified or not, it is terribly real to the individuals living it. The feeling deserves respect. It also deserves assurances that one's faith is not in jeopardy. I resonate with what N. T. Wright stated in *The Last Word: Scripture and the Authority of God — Getting Beyond the Bible Wars*:

> [H]istory should hold no terrors for the Christian. . . It might be better to believe without seeing, as Jesus said to Thomas on that occasion; but for those who have asked the skeptic's question, Christianity should be ready to give an answer about what really happened within history and how, within the historian's own proper discipline, we can know that with the kind of "knowledge" appropriate to, and available within, historical research."[1]

Wright makes the further point,

> In addressing the question, we might discover things about what scripture is saying which our own traditions had conveniently screened out. Perhaps. . . we will get down to the task we should never have abandoned, that of continually trying to understand and live by our foundation texts even better than our predecessors. Again, that is precisely what living by the authority of scripture looks like in practice.[2]

There may be some serious shepherding to be done with some of the frightened flock, but I contend that deep scriptural familiarity and study are essential to the very health, wellbeing, and courage of the flock.

The other manifestation of seeming resistance I've encountered is really a manifestation of an individual's hunger for knowing, a hunger that has neither been recognized by church leadership nor fed sufficiently within the local church setting. What I hear in this case are direct statements such as, "I'd have been active [in a local church] long before if I knew the Bible held all this!" and "How long have we [meaning scholars, professors, authors, the pastor, et al.] known about this? Since at least the 1940's? In some cases earlier? Why weren't we [meaning congregation members in general and the questioner in specific] told? I'd have stayed involved if I'd had a chance to learn about this." Here is something more subtle, not resistance to learning but skepticism about the ability of organized religion to deliver deep substance. Here is a protest against the institution and its leadership for settling for the dry, under-stimulating, over-simplified version of the faith that it presented week in and week out year after year. It turns into inadvertent resistance toward the local church and engagement with the life of the local church. The looming tragedy is that this skepticism about the ability of organized religion to deliver deep substance often leads to wholesale turning away from the church, in effect throwing the baby out with the bathwater, which in turn leads to despair. Despair of the intellect, despair of the soul.

Like diners who have been regulars at a restaurant, they discover they must change their meal choices in order to stay strong and healthy. But the restaurant menu stays the same. So the diners quit that restaurant and all others of that ilk. They give up on dining out, choosing instead to cook for themselves, tackling rigorous recipes from diverse and challenging sources. It is difficult to persuade them to try a restaurant again. The despair is that real, yet it usually goes unrecognized by the chefs who are the church leadership, primarily because no one asks the question, "What do you need in order to be spiritually fed?"

The question I want to pose, though placed in terms of potential resistance to biblical literacy, is not about whether that resistance will make our attempts at biblical literacy futile, but how we can turn it to something fertile.

Talk to Me[3]

It was March in Myrtle Beach, South Carolina, Day Four of a five-day seminar I was leading on Christian education for the twenty-first century. The group of twenty-two comprised mostly clergy, along with four clergy spouses and four laymen. Two of the laymen were new this year, specially invited by their pastors who were long-time participants. The clergy were United Church of Christ and United Methodists, most actively serving local congregations as solo pastors though at least two were senior pastors of multiple-staff churches. One of the clergy was a woman. The parishes served ranged from small to large, from rural to suburban to urban, in Ohio, Illinois, and North Dakota. Several of the now-retired clergy had begun attending the Myrtle Beach seminar some thirty years ago while actively serving as local church pastors and conference staff. Two of the laymen had been coming for over fifteen years, and had formed fast friendships among themselves and my husband, the seminar's coordinator. Over the past nine or ten years, as their wives and I intermittently appeared for the seminar, the six of us became good friends.

This was the fifth or sixth year I'd been with the group, the second as its seminar leader. I was back as leader at the group's invitation, and because of their desire and willingness to tackle some major issues in the arena of Christian education and educational ministries at this twenty-first century point in the life of the church in general and their congregations in particular. Except for the new participants, I knew everyone and everyone knew me. We'd learned together, had shared intensely candid discussions on church life, leadership, and ministry, and had eaten many meals together. We had laughed and joked, sung and worshipped together. I tell you all this because I want you to have a sense of the group and the deeply collegial environment of the seminar.

On Day One of the Seminar I had provided an overview of the week's topics. When I gave the title "Congregational Biblical (Il)literacy: The Cost of Pastor's Secret Knowledge," every clergyperson around the tables nodded, a kind of determined look crossing each face. It was the only topic to elicit that kind of response.

At the end of Day Three's session I reminded the group that "tomorrow" we'd be focusing on "Congregational Biblical (Il)literacy: The Cost of Pastor's Secret Knowledge." Again nods all around, this time with determined looks accompanied by anticipation.

That afternoon, as I reviewed what I'd planned for the Pastor's Secret Knowledge session, I kept returning to the image of my colleagues' nods and expressions. If I was reading the body language correctly, they were resonating with the topic, genuinely anticipating the chance to explore it and deal with it. But what else lay behind those nodding heads and determined looks?

To move forward with the session as I'd originally planned suddenly seemed presumptuous. I had expected them to respond with curiosity about "secret knowledge," curiosity about what I meant and into what I was going to lead them. I was prepped for that session. It was the determined looks that kept throwing me. Like they knew there was bitter medicine awaiting them and that they were going to stand in place and make themselves receive it.

I reorganized the session, setting parts aside, tweaking others. The most significant change was the beginning of the session itself.

Day Four arrived. Morning worship and other "housekeeping" announcements were completed. Leadership was turned over to me.

I told the group what I'd observed throughout the week each time I'd mentioned today's topic. I described the expressions that came onto their faces: the nodding of heads, the kind of determined anticipation. Then I moved out from behind the podium, spread my hands and said, "Talk to me. Why have so many of your heads been nodding knowingly whenever I mention the cost of pastors' secret knowledge?"

And they did. They spoke of small attendance at Bible study. They spoke of their weeks getting gobbled up by church maintenance emergencies, hospital calls, newsletter deadlines, confirmation class, worship bulletin preparation, committee and board meetings, deaths in the congregation, sermon writing, denominational and community involvements. They spoke of church members' weeks getting gobbled up.

They spoke of efforts made and small successes. They spoke of lay leaders with wonderful nurturing skills when it came to helping others engage in biblical study. They spoke of piloting the integration of scripture into the broader life of the church.

One told the story of a pastor in the Midwest who conducted what he called The World's Shortest Bible Study every Sunday morning in the fifteen minutes before worship. Seems he held it right in the sanctuary where, of course, the people were gathering. He used the overflow exegetical materials from his sermon preparation. The choir members rehearsed during the regular education hour, so this was a way to capture some faith formation time for them while they were already in the building. It also captured anyone who arrived just those few minutes earlier for worship.

Another pastor, looking sheepish, confided that he just didn't know how to go about taking what he'd learned in seminary and transforming it into accessible forms for his adults.

A third said, "If I tried to talk about the Bible the way I know it and what I know about it, they'd fire me." That started an entirely new line of conversation about conflicting viewpoints and interpretations of scripture even within the same denomination or tradition, and what the pastor's responsibility was, as a called minister of the gospel, to stand firm in the face of biblical illiteracy in all its varied forms. They were looking biblical illiteracy and their culpability for its continuation straight in the eye.

Then one of the laymen at the table said with a mix of enthusiasm and awe, "I'm sitting here and I'm thinking 'I had no idea that any of this stuff [content of discussion] even existed.' I can't wait to find out what you're all referring to about the Bible." Then he turned to his own pastor, who was seated next to him, and asked enthusiastically, "When are we going to start?"

Important Work: Naming Frustrations and Obstacles

How and where will each of you start the important work of naming the frustrations and obstacles, the small or large successes, the constraints and the fears you live with in relation to congregational biblical illiteracy and your biblical "secret knowledge?" Recall that I could turn to the group at the Myrtle Beach seminar and say, "Talk to me," because we already had a strong trust relationship. As a group they had covenanted together for years to keep within the group what was shared in that seminar. It was a safe environment. Tough and touchy subjects could be seriously raised and discussed.

It was different when I led a conference-wide event on congregational biblical illiteracy and the cost of pastor's "secret knowledge." It was different in part because I did not know them and they did not know me. We did the exercise "What Secret Knowledge" (see above), which was literally exercise for some as they stood up and sat down in response to the various survey prompts. On the worksheet the next item was "Naming the Obstacles and the Frustrations." At that point I said, "I don't know you, and you don't know me. This is a task to be done among or within a group that has a significant degree of trust in one another and the facilitator so that it is safe to take the risks inherent in being candid."

That is what I say to you as well. Do the naming of obstacles and frustrations relative to biblical literacy among or within a collegial group in which there is a significant degree of trust in one another, so that it is safe to take the risks inherent in being candid. Of course you can do the naming of obstacles and frustrations on your own. If we are thoroughly honest with ourselves we will discover that not all the obstacles lie in the laity's court, nor can all our frustrations be traced to someone else's stonewalling or deeds left undone. We protect ourselves by defaulting to our laments about who and what stand in our way of real Bible literacy. Reporting our obstacles and frustrations within a trusted circle that has covenanted to keep one another honest and accountable has several distinct advantages. One is that the actual articulation of obstacles and frustrations plaguing you has a better chance of happening. A second is that, in having to clarify for others what you mean, you can become more aware of what experiences you are trying to express. A third is that you are less likely to get away with the figurative cattle manure in place of authentic self and situation analysis.

Why bother with the step of naming obstacles and frustrations? We do it in order to acknowledge their existence. We do it to record that which we've acknowledged. Most importantly, we do it to break the repetitive loop we've created that keeps us cycling back over and over again through the obstacles and frustrations, spinning our wheels as it were, instead of digging in, finding traction, and moving ourselves and our local congregants forward. The essential point is that you *do it*. Merry-go-rounds and ferries wheels are great for amusement parks and carnivals. The vital congregation needs leadership equipped for off-road exploration. Name the time crunches, the potential and long-suffering conflicts and their champions, the lack of ecclesiastical hierarchy support, the work it will take. Clear the way for making changes, do something, put yourself in gear.

Many years ago I remember being at the annual meeting of my denomination's world ministries board of directors. The chronic complaint of the local church pastors who served on the board of directors revolved around the annual budgeting process of their churches. Seems the local church governing boards typically decided how much they thought the members of the church would be able to give any particular year and fashioned the budgets around that amount. The pastors then found themselves in an uncomfortable position between denominational support, including world mission, and their own salaries. If they advocated increasing denominational support, there was no money for a salary increase. If they accepted a salary increase, denominational support would not be raised. I heard two responses in the small group sessions that have stuck with me ever since. One was from Rev. Scott Libby, then the Conference Minister for the United Church of Christ's Iowa Conference. What I remember him saying was basically, "I tell all the pastors new to the Iowa Conference, 'You go after Our Church's Wider Mission and I'll go after your salary for you.' They do, and I do. The body of Christ gains all around."

The other response was from a local church pastor serving a small church in a small town. My guess was that his salary was about the same as mine, which was small even for that time. He said that any time the decision came down to increasing denominational mission support or raising his salary he told the church council, "There's no question — we increase our giving to others. You'll all know if my family and I have extenuating needs, and I know you'll take care of us. But who will take care of others around the country and around the world if we don't? They are our responsibility as faithful Christians."

Why do these two comments still help inform my ministry? I think because they generate traction instead of fueling our spinning tires. I have an intriguing strategy that can help get you and your local congregation started in biblical literacy that I'll share in just a moment. Before that, I want to turn once more to something N. T. Wright wrote in *The Last Word: Scripture and the Authority of God — Getting Beyond the Bible Wars* that has some bearing on our reluctance to engage seriously and systematically in Biblical literacy with our congregations. Wright confronts fundamental and progressive Christian alike about why we don't want to encounter scripture as "critical realists" and don't want to move beyond the literal/non-literal polarization. The picture isn't especially pretty.

> The fact that I have criticized the "literal/non-literal" polarization does not mean that I am indifferent to the question of whether the events written about in the gospels actually took place. Far from it. It is just that it will not do to repeat irrelevant slogans and imagine that one has thereby settled the matter. There is a great gulf fixed between those who want to prove the historicity of everything reported in the Bible in order to demonstrate that the Bible is "true" after all and those who, committed to living under the authority of scripture remain open to what scripture itself actually teaches and emphasizes. Which is the bottom line: "proving the Bible to be true" (often with the effect of saying, "*So we can go on thinking what we've always thought*") or taking it *so seriously that we allow it to tell us things we'd never heard before and didn't particularly want to hear?*[4]

Biblical literacy takes work. Biblical literacy requires investing ourselves in study, in dialogue, in questing for the word that God would reveal to us through God's word. If a congregation is to be vital, its vitality will derive from and be sustained by ever more intentional "taking seriously" of Holy Scripture through the necessary and ever surprising work with that scripture in all its nuances and depth.

Now, here's the intriguing strategy that can help you and your congregation get biblical literacy started.

The Biblical Illiteracy Reduction Snowball

A local United Methodist church offered a twelve-week course based on Dave Ramsey's book *Financial Peace Revisited*> last year and our two grown sons signed up for it[5] Each Sunday evening, if they were at our house, I'd pump them for tips on budgeting, on saving money for different purposes from emergency to vacation, and on debt management. My husband David and I have experienced fluctuations in our incomes every twelve to twenty-four months due to David's calling as an intentional interim minister. Sometimes the ministries were part time, other times full time. We also had loaned ourselves (through a home equity loan) the money to add a deck and screened porch to our small house. I was ready for a different strategy.

Of the various strategies and worksheets my sons shared with me, the one that caught my full attention was the Debt Snowball.[6] The goal is to become debt-free. As my sons explained it, the strategy is to put all your debts in a list from smallest to largest, without regard to interest rate. Everything goes on the list that's a debt — credit cards, mortgages, home equity loans, student loans, medical bills, car payments, and so forth — even if there's only one payment left. Each month you pay the minimum amount due or the set payment amount (like with a car loan), except for the debt at the top of the list. With that one, the smallest debt, you pay the minimum plus any other extra dollars you'd been putting toward the others beyond the minimum. If everything else was already on minimum payment, then add whatever you can from elsewhere in your spending even if it's just a dollar or two in order to begin paying down the balance of the first debt.

Okay, so far nothing really new is going on here except for ignoring the interest rate. It's when the first debt gets paid off that the strategy ramps up. As soon as Debt #1 is paid off, you take the monthly amount you used to use for it and add it — all of it — to Debt #2's minimum or set payment. That combined amount becomes Debt #2's monthly payment. Continue to follow the plan through the complete payoff of Debt #2: (1) pay the larger amount each month, (2) pay all the other minimums or set amounts each month, (3) do not make purchases that will add new debt. If you are tempted to just put a little more into some other debt further down the list, resist! Add it to Debt #2's payment instead, and don't just spend it either!

Each time you pay off the last of a debt, you start a new worksheet. It doesn't sound like much, but I can tell you from experience that writing up a new worksheet, putting a huge smiley face on the retiring one and stapling the old one behind the new one is a joyful moment. Why? Because you re-calculate the number of payments you'll have to make on Debt #3 based on the new monthly amount you bring to it: Debt #1 monthly payment + Debt #2 monthly payment + Debt #3 minimum or set payment. Whereas originally Debt #3 was going to take, let's say, a few years to pay off, now it's going to take less time — sometimes significantly less time. Then Debt #3's enlarged payment amount will get rolled into Debt #4's minimum, and so on and so on. The debt snowball rolls down the list, gaining substance and momentum, cleaning up each debt as it goes.

Local congregations and church leaders need to put themselves on a biblical debt snowball. The debt we owe is in the coinage of biblical literacy. We are so far in debt that we're nearly bankrupt.

N. T. Wright reminds us that:

> The Western church has for some generations allowed a dangerous "separation of powers," according to which scripture is taught by professional academics while the church is run by clergy who, with noble exceptions, rely on secondhand and increasingly outdated understandings of scripture itself. . . The result is not only a deep impoverishment, but a creeping or even galloping bureaucratization, as church leaders engage in displacement activities, hoping to do through committees, filing cabinets and legal constraints what they should be doing through prayerful, powerful biblical preaching, teaching and pastoral work.[7]

Think for a minute about what we pastors and church educators are costing the people we serve, and by implication the body of Christ, by keeping our biblical knowledge "secret" and keeping biblical illiteracy going. What kind of faith formation opportunities and nurturing appear out of reach because all that local churches have been willing to do for years was pay the minimum due while investing nothing toward reducing the principle of the biblical illiteracy debt? Here are a few of the costs we've run up. I expect you will add others from your own experiences and insights.

• Only childhood knowledge of a few basic Bible stories.

   Key, but basic because they are never placed within the overarching narrative

Key, but basic because the deeper, richer, more complex levels of the stories — the levels that truly engage us in an encounter with the transcendent God and that have the power to challenge, reconcile, redeem, and transform us — are never explored or experienced

- Assumptions that the laity aren't interested or don't care, which lead to . . .
No authentic partnership in the community of faith. They remain at the worker bee level

  Unhealthy, dependent parent-child relationships in which the child is neither allowed to grow up and participate in and shoulder the full adulthood realities (some joyful, some disconcerting) nor mentored into full adulthood by those in the parent role (i.e., pastors). Either way leads to a patronization or condemnation of the laity by the biblically trained pastors.

- Assumptions that congregants are not capable of learning, understanding, and applying the historical, contextual and cultural, let alone the theological realities behind and within the scriptural texts. Such an assumption leads to attitudes of condescension.

Let us be mindful that Jesus worked with fishermen first, teaching, modeling, mentoring, correcting, and trusting them as full partners in the words of good news he brought, and in the fashioning of God's realm of wholeness, social equity, and justice for all people and all creation. Few if any of us ordained clergy, lay ministers, and Christian educators began our formal educational scripture endeavors with more than a rudimentary Sunday School level of familiarity. For us, everything was new and much of it was totally unexpected. Even the familiar changed as we encountered the linguistic, historical, cultural, socio-political, and theological dynamics at work in the story (actually, stories) of creation, the Twenty-Third Psalm, the work of Isaiah (all three of them), the narratives of Jesus' birth, the procession of Jesus and the crowd into Jerusalem just days before his death.

Our biblical knowledge, kept secret, can cost the followers of Christ and the potential followers of Christ:

- knowledge, belief, conviction, even faith itself
- resources to meet challenges and make challenges
- authentic reason to live their lives differently and to be genuinely part of something much larger than themselves that can make all the difference in the global village in which they live

- the foundation to challenge the powers of empire and social injustice
- comfort and succor in times of distress, strife, and diminishing hope
- full partnership in God's realm and full participation in God's salvation history unfolding daily

Finally, what does our knowledge-kept-secret cost the people of God? It withholds from them their birthright as God's people

- to know God most fully through the transcendent Word
- to act in concert with that Word for the healing of the nations and all creation

Before you start accusing me of utopian thinking, let me remind you that I know most people aren't flocking or even straggling to Bible studies. I know you have in some way or another tried to keep faith with the teaching of scripture in your congregational settings and that few of you have had much resounding success either numerically (lots of people) or substantively (quality study transforming at least small groups of people). Looking across the years and local church congregations I've served, I have to admit to having engaged in Bible study groups that were small in attendance — consistent but small — and that did not seem to impact the lives of those who came. Put into a formula, such a track record looks like "quality exegetical exploration of various books of the Bible + consistent participation = unknown impact." Coupling my track record with what I'll call entrenched biblical illiteracy across those congregations and so many others is causing me to rethink the how and wherefore of local church scriptural study. It is into this rethinking mode that I invite you to join me now.

From Secret Knowledge to Communal Knowledge

Keep these words that I am commanding you today in your heart. Recite them to your children and when you lie down and when you are at home and when you are away, when you lie down and when you rise. (Deuteronomy 6:6–7.)

Churches overestimate what they can do in one year and underestimate what they can do in five years.[8]

89

Example of one biblical literacy goal: That each member will participate in a study of scripture each year, with the goal of accumulating familiarity with and expanded understanding of our sacred texts. Three periods — fall, winter, summer. Multiple approaches: (1) Gospel for next lectionary season, (2) . . . [9]

So, what kind of strategies do we need to transform the secret knowledge to communal knowledge? One size isn't going to fit all. Neither is one type suitable for the varying contexts within congregations. The strategies discussed below offer a place and a way to start the biblical illiteracy snowball. Keep doing the "minimum" on most Bible-related efforts, which might be simply sustaining what's already in place. Meanwhile, rather than throwing additional energy in several directions at once, focus extra energy on one . . . the smallest or easiest to enlarge . . . to reduce the biblical illiteracy debt in that one area. When that first "debt" is paid off, as in established and working well, then tackle a second effort. But first, let's get that starter snowball made.

Simply Starting Simply

The Worship Bulletin
Carve out a section in the printed worship bulletin for background on one or more of the books from which the scripture of the day is taken. Include possible dates of origin and written form, circumstances surrounding the events narrated in the book, and how the book fits in to the overall flow of the biblical narrative.

- If scripture passages from the same book are used for a number of weeks, add information as the weeks go on.
- When texts relate to each other, offer background information highlighting the different historical and religious contexts of each (e.g., dates of origination, the original audience and their circumstances) as well as what links the texts together (e.g., a gospel account of Jesus quoting that Hebrew scripture, a theological theme resonating in both scriptures).
- Use a brief timeline of biblical events, including dates and some other historical markers to help place the events in the wider arena of the ancient world.
- Include a map once in a while, pointing out the geographical locations relevant to the scriptures of the day. Add details to help worshippers acclimate to such things as the distance between places, why a location had a special

significance, and so forth. For instance, when Jesus walks from the Galilee to Jerusalem it would be about equal to walking from _____ to _____ (fill in local town or county names).

Pew Racks

Add some of the items suggested for the worship bulletin to the pew racks if you have them. Especially useful for repeated reference would be a timeline of biblical events and maps of several different time periods. The strategy is then to call worshippers' attention to the timeline and maps in relation to the day's scripture lessons. This does not mean the flow of worship needs to be compromised. Think creatively. Remember the local church pastor, mentioned earlier, who does The World's Shortest Bible Study in a fifteen-minute segment before the prelude to each worship service. If biblical literacy is the priority, you'll come up with ways to foster it.

Your Ideas

Those of you who are pastors and professional church educators have the educational background to assemble the pieces discussed above and to think of other strategies to add or substitute. But you aren't the only ones in your congregation who could research and assemble this kind of basic biblical background. With a good reference book like *Harper Collins Bible Dictionary*,[10] a textbook that introduces the Hebrew Bible and the New Testament, an introductory survey book such as a Study Bible or The Pilgrim Press' *Bible for Vital Congregations* by Barbara J. Essex,[11] an interested layperson, youth group, or confirmation class could provide this ministry. Think what a learning experience it would be for them!

You don't have to be the sole idea-generator either. You do need to be clear about the goals and intentions. The important thing to remember is that every strategy that's put into place builds the snowball. The bigger the snowball, the more impact you and congregation have already had on biblical illiteracy.

Point-in-Time Exercise: Simply Starting Simply

■ Identify at least two Simply Starting Simply strategies to pilot in your local church, then for each one jot down: (1) the responsible party at the beginning, (2) the responsible party/parties for continuing the strategy, (3) supplies needed, and (4) approvals needed. Now you've got something concrete with which to begin!

Note: there's a worksheet on www.thepilgrimpress for your use.

GPS (Good Pastoral Suggestions) for Navigating Secular and Christian Bookstores

Publication of books on religion and spirituality has increased exponentially in recent years. Walk into any large bookstore and you will find shelves upon shelves of books covering spirituality, religions of the world including Christianity, prayer and meditation, devotions, themes in the Bible, women and men in the Bible, novels based on biblical narratives, and various translations and paraphrases of the Holy Bible. Walk into Christian bookstores and the shelves overflow with even more. In both cases there are sections for adults, youth, and children's materials. Visit online booksellers and the story is the same.

Don't simply send people to the bookstores without GPS — Good Pastoral Suggestions. As with any market, some wares will be more helpful than others. Some wares will be packaged in eye-catching, interest-piquing ways. Those may or may not be as nurturing or edifying as they first appear. There are denominational, non-denominational, and independent presses that reflect theology, biblical traditions, and church practices all across the continuum of Christianity. Pastors and church educators need to be proactive with their faith communities. They can do this by providing helpful navigational guidelines for finding books and authors that challenge and nurture within their tradition, as well as identifying how books and authors outside their tradition fit within Christianity's continuum of beliefs and practices. For example, pointing people toward publishers and authors you trust biblically and away from those that run counter to your tradition is a straightforward navigational guideline.

When I'm looking through an unfamiliar publisher's Study Bible, Bible dictionary, or commentary, I use the treatment of Genesis and Revelation as a quick litmus test. If the information about the creation narratives in Genesis 1–3 speaks of six 24-hour days after which God rested for the seventh 24-hour day and about a specific geographical location for the Garden of Eden, I know it is written from a literalist theological and biblical perspective. The same is true if the commentary speaks of Revelation's texts as predictions of what will happen in our future rather than images and messages that gave hope to Christians persecuted to death during the Roman Emperor Domitian's reign. On the other hand, if the Study Bible, Bible dictionary, or commentary explains the situation under which Christians were suffering during

Domitian's rule, the message of hope the author of Revelation offered, and the use of images and symbols that would not look "anti-Roman" and therefore not compromise the safety of someone "caught" with this book, I know the non-literalist perspective is present.

Don't have time to visit bookstores online or on the ground? No bookstore near you? No internet service available? There's always the old fashioned way. Call or write to several colleagues. Explain what you're pulling together. List what you've got so far. Ask them to add up to five titles and/or guidelines. Tell them you'll put a master list together and send them copies. Surprise! You've just created your Model A GPS for bookstores and libraries.

Point-in-Time Exercise: GPS for Bookstores

■ Using the chart available on www.thepilgrimpress.com, list at least one guideline and one recommended book under each category in the chart. What might a guideline include? Something like "good, readable overview" or "If you are reading _____ then balance it with _____" could get you started. Then take it from there.

Make the most of your GPS.

• Remember to update the GPS lists whenever you find something better.
• Does the church have a bulletin board? Post the GPS and update it seasonally.
• Turn it into a wallet size card — like a double-fold business card — and make it available in pews or at the welcome/hospitality center.
• Does the church have a web site? Post your GPS on it, and update it seasonally.
• Display sample books from the recommendation list where visitors, friends, and members can notice and peruse them.
• Consider hosting an in-house book sale and/or book swap ministry.

Remember, not everyone's first choice is books. The same type of GPS is needed for videos and DVDs available at public libraries, movie rentals, online and on-ground stores. Many of these began as television episodes or series on PBS, the History Channel, and the Discovery Channel. Now they are available to the public.

Point-in-Time Exercise: GPS for Movies and TV

▓ Using the chart available on www.thepilgrimpress.com, list at least one guideline and one recommended movie or television episode/series for each category. A guideline might state something like "explores archaeological discoveries relevant to biblical sites" or "provocative discussion of narratives in the book of Genesis." Add or delete categories as needed. Think about your audience and their needs. You'll notice I included several of my personal favorites.

There are also songs, hymns, and major choral works that deal with the Bible and biblical themes. In this instance think of your GPS list as a play list or Top 10 list for your iPod. Remember, some people will not be familiar with the pieces you think everyone knows, nor will they be familiar with any particular significance of the piece. I've often thought how totally cool it would be to spend a worship year preaching from the scriptural texts in Handel's *Messiah*. There would easily be enough for Advent, Christmas, Epiphany, then through to Lent, Easter, and beyond. Not quite sure what I'd do with Chorus #37 "The Lord gave the word: great was the company of the preachers," especially when the Soprano Air immediately following is about beautiful feet, but I'd figure out something well rounded biblically and contemporarily insightful (I hope). Once again, there's a chart available on www.thepilgrimpress.com for your use. I've included a few of my favorites there, too. Now it's your turn.

As prolific as are authors in print, even more prolific are sites on the internet. Consider creating a GPS that provides guidance to sites with reliable information. In the case of websites you might want to include a caution section to alert your people to opinion sites in contrast with scholarship sites, subjective postings in contrast to more objective informational postings. Students in the biblical courses I teach often find sites they think are providing scholarship but are actually papers and presentations posted by other college students or individual pastors. There are all kinds of material on the Web, much of it looking reputable. If you want to move those in your local church toward biblical literacy, give them a GPS even for the Web.

Point-in-Time Exercise: GPS for the Web

▓ I know, I know . . . you know the drill! Check out the chart on www.thepilgrimpress.com for this exercise, and then go ahead and list at least one guideline and one recommended web site for each category. Add or delete categories as needed. Think about your audience and their needs. You may not be surfing the Web for Bible information, but that doesn't mean others in the congregation aren't. That includes the youth and children who may have friends pointing them toward sites that the friends' pastors and teachers have shown them. I haven't included any of mine this time because unlike books and movies that remain in a physically accessible form, websites and links can change frequently out of necessity.

Feeling a little overwhelmed? Be not dismayed. Embarking on a long-neglected literacy project is a little like tackling the renovation of a long-neglected but once beloved old house. It certainly takes effort. When it comes to our Holy Scriptures, the effort of this renovation is our calling as church leaders, ordained and non-ordained, church professionals and laity.

Once again, you do not have to do any of this alone. Collaborate with colleagues. Recruit a team of church members to work on any of these projects. Just don't do nothing. It's easy to complain. Don't be the one who says, "I don't want to work that hard" on something this important.

Bigger Investment, Bigger Gains or Getting the Parents Onboard

So far the strategies suggested are straightforward and relatively easy to implement. You've got a nice snowball going. Bringing lay leadership on board will vary from congregation to congregation. You'll make adaptations for your context as you pilot strategies and discover or create other strategies that will fit the needs of your local church even better.

What about strategies for beginning biblical literacy at younger ages? Church school curricular resources familiarize children with major biblical narratives. Yet colleagues continue to report that young people coming into confirmation bring little knowledge and less understanding of the Bible as a whole, the Bible as a library of books that span over a thousand years of history, or the Bible as the sacred narratives of faith based in a covenant initiated by God.

I want to suggest a radically new approach: the use of parental informed consent at about the time young people move into sixth grade. Schools do it for sex education. They send information to homes about the curriculum to be used, invite parents to come to the school and read through the materials, and require that an informed consent form be signed and returned to the school indicating whether or not the child is permitted to participate in the sex education program. We can do the same for Bible education that going to take the young people beyond the simple repetition of major Bible stories they have known to this point.

Why sixth grade? Several reasons. Young people are old enough to work with different types of literature. They know from school about fiction and non-fiction. They are familiar with science and history, biography and autobiography. They're learning about opinion pieces such as letters to the editor and the editor's column in newspapers, commentaries on television, and wikis and blogs on the Web. They've had to write reports, book reviews, poems, essays, and short stories. They know the difference between fictional heroes (e.g., The Fantastic Four, Nancy Drew, the Hulk, Indiana Jones, Luke and Leia Skywalker, Harry Potter, Hermione Granger, Lucy and Susan of Narnia) and real-life heroes (e.g., Rosa Parks, Sally Ride, Wilma Rudolph, Marian Wright Edelman, Martin Luther King, Jr., Gandhi, Neil Armstrong).

Sixth graders have seen sport and Hollywood stars rise and fall, and they're beginning to understand that even our best examples of humanity have imperfections. At the same time they often are not aware of some of the contradictory behind-the-scenes attitudes and activities of those they admire; nor are their parents. So there's naiveté but it's mixed with growing awareness and expanding ability to evaluate and provide commentary on both the public façade and the less public reality.

Sixth graders have a developing historical sense. They understand years, centuries and millennia. They recognize differences in various historical cultures as well as variations between cultures of the same time period. A good example of the latter is their ability to research and report on the culture of the Northern and the Southern States leading up to the American Civil War.

Sixth graders function extremely well when they experience themselves at the top of the elementary ladder rather than at the bottom of the middle school or junior high ladder. The local church can enhance the sixth graders' experience by creating a Christian faith formation environment that initiates these young people into the grown-up world of biblical exploration during this critical year. Of course they will be novices. That's the way we all began. Just make sure the years that follow continue the stretching and nurturing of their new-found relationship with scripture.

Why the Informed Parental Consent? Oh, some of you thought I was joking! No, I'm serious. The most straightforward reason is respect for the parents who, after all, entrust their young people to the church for faith formation — especially anything to do with the Bible.

Requiring a signed Informed Parental Consent for sixth graders' study of scripture sends a clear message to the parents that the church leadership takes the complexities of scripture and the study of scripture seriously. No more retelling of well-worn simplified Bible stories. The sixth graders are moving from Little League to the Minors.

A second reason is that parents need a chance for their questions to be answered before their children begin. Parents deserve to *not* be blindsided. You may need to address fears about "what you'll teach them." I suspect any fears will be grounded in worries that (a) the children will know more than the parents, or (b) the children will be taught something the parents believe is wrong or false. The "wrong" or "false" teaching fear may best be handled in conversation with parents in order to determine to what they are referring. You are then more able to address those specific concerns.

How much opposition will you face? In reality, probably not much, unless there is a significant discrepancy between the congregation's and your biblical and theological positions. The parents in all likelihood will be curious about the Bible, too. This, then, is a third reason for the Informed Parental Consent. You may have the happy problem of needing to run parallel parent sessions or parent + sixth grader gatherings in which the children become mentors to the parents. This could certainly answer "(a)" above.

When I think about how much life-giving, life-shaping, life-sustaining, and life-saving awaits us in scripture, I don't want to waste those precious formative sixth- through ninth-grade years. If anyone needed scriptural equipping for the secular and spiritual journey, these young people need it desperately. Let's not waste that sixth grade. Let's not keep these almost adolescents at a child's level at church while leaving them on their own as they are bombarded with adult-size images, life-styles, and pressures day in and day out. They need a life-and-soul alternative big enough, grown-up enough, deep enough, unconditionally loving and steadfast enough to stand up against what's coming at them. To borrow from Home Depot's slogan, "They can do it. We can help."

Point-in-Time Exercise: Informed Parental Consent for Biblical Study

▓ Draft an informational notice to parents of incoming sixth graders. Briefly explain the Bible education program in which their children will be engaged. Explain the Informed Parental Consent for Biblical Study included with the notice. Invite them to attend one of the orientation chats. Provide a due date for returning the signed consent form. Keep the draft for future reference.

Why a draft before anything else is done? Consider it a way to focus on the objective. By drafting the informational notice, you will have to think through some of the details for making the strategy a reality. All the details don't need to go into the notice, even in its final form. But you should have a clear and comfortable vision and be able to convey it succinctly to the parents. Doing your first draft now gives you something to bounce off of later in the process.

▓ List the steps necessary to shift from the current sixth grade curricular model to one integrating intentional Bible education. For example, will a new curricular resource be needed or will better use of the current one work as well? What would "better use" mean specifically?

▓ For each step, include any approvals needed in order to move forward smoothly, plus a tentative timetable. For example, once you bring the idea to the Christian education committee, and assuming they favor the plan, will the church's governing board need only to hear a report about it, or will that board have to vote on it also? Will there be informal conversations with parents before anything specific is done?

▓ Make use of the worksheet on www.thepilgrimpress.com to track your thinking, to communicate your ideas to others, and to involve others in the process as it develops into the full strategy for sixth-grade Bible education with informed parental consent.

A colleague on Defiance College's religion faculty, Dean Johnson, closes his emails with a single word: imagine. Imagine the biblical literacy that can take hold and replace the biblical illiteracy that once pervaded the life of the congregation. Imagine . . . the snowball you and the congregation created together has reduced the biblical illiteracy debt, and you will have a snowman of biblical proportions to show for it!

Biblical Literacy: The Joy of Pastors' Knowledge Shared

I'll finish this chapter by coming full circle back to the scriptures with which I began.

> Your word is a lamp to my feet and a light to my path. (Psalm 119:105.)
>
> No one after lighting a lamp puts it under a bushel basket, but on a lamp stand, and it gives light to all in the house. (Matthew 5:15.)

At the Christmas Eve candlelight services of some churches, everyone receives the challenge to carry their individual candles home still lighted, bringing the Light of the World anew into their hearth and hearts. I've witnessed the great glee adults and children alike radiate as they carefully help one another maneuver into winter coats and gloves, make their way to the outer doors of the building, and protect the candle's flame from winter's breath. They are passionate that the light not go out. Families often sacrifice one or two flames in order to collectively keep another alive. One year we managed to get four out the church door, two safely to the car, and one safely into the house. Watching our two junior high sons strategize together and then successfully carry out the teamwork that brought success to the mission was one of those sacred moments of space and time.

I urge you, yea I beseech you, to make ways in your local congregation to share the biblical knowledge and training you have as a pastor or professional church educator. Take the bushel basket off of your lighted lamp. Did you notice that there is so much light being hidden it took a bushel basket to contain it? Let the people in on the fact that there is *so much* that can be tapped into, and that you'll get them started. Let the secret out that "God has yet more light and truth to break forth from God's Word."[20]

At one time the ritual of passing the flame from the Christ candle to individual candles did not exist. Yet now many of us cannot imagine a Christmas Eve service without it. The simple act of first receiving and then giving the flame, and then the personal and communal experience of sinking into darkness that is yet aglow with light, bring transcendence.

Work with the people of God whom you serve and create those simple acts of giving what you have already received — that incredible biblical light and knowledge that so far you've kept so "secret." Be ready to receive from the people as well, as the depth and rich sustenance of God's Word is shared.

For where the Holy Scripture is studied and explored, and where lives are challenged, enriched, and strengthened in the simple acts of studying and exploring scripture, there transcendence is also.

Five

Learning to Fish or Settling
for Buying the Catch of the Day

Example from the Field: "To Market to Market to Buy a Fat
. . . VBS Curricular Resource"

Staci and Abby, two local church Directors of Christian Education, decided to go to a Vacation Bible School curriculum showcase several Februarys ago. Their congregations had committed to doing joint Vacation Bible School again that year. The young women wanted to see what materials were going to be available, then determine which best suited the churches' needs. I found out about their plans to attend the showcase when Staci, who was taking a Christian education course with me that semester, mentioned it. Abby had taken similar courses with me previously, plus she was serving the church I attend and was, therefore, my colleague and "my DCE" to whom I turned for wisdom and counsel when it came to the life and ministry of that local church. So when Staci mentioned the planned showcase I was intrigued.

Several weeks later Staci reported on the experience. Yes, it was successful. Yes, there had been a number of curricular resources from which to choose. Each publisher's representative had about fifteen minutes to show and explain their material. Staci explained how various representatives led off with "Here's the theme, here are the games, and the music, and the crafts, and the snacks that go with the theme." She said, "They showed us all the promotion items and decorating items and CDs and DVD clips and talked about how much fun the kids would have. Then at the very end of their presenting time they added what biblical basis or Bible stories were included. It was like the Bible stories and teachings were an afterthought or just the excuse to develop all the other jazzy stuff." She went on to explain that only one actually began by discussing what the biblical basis for the curriculum was, what stories were included, why those stories were chosen, and what the publisher hoped the children would learn through that VBS program. Then that publisher rep walked the audience quickly through the supplementary materials. Staci added candidly, "If Abby and I hadn't known about assessing curriculum resources, we could easily have been impressed by all the 'fun stuff' and never known if there was any substance in the curriculum or not." Then she said, "Know which material we ended up choosing? The one whose rep explained the biblical basis and goals first before ever mentioning the other stuff. It really helped that we both knew how to look for what was important for the children's faith first rather than what just looked like 'Oh this will be fun.'"

There is a plethora of commercially produced resources for every possible manner of ministry imaginable in the local church. Some are excellent, some are just awful. Some are well grounded in theology and educational theory and practice; many are not. The glitzy, easy-to-use curricular resources, while they frequently draw the eye and ignite enthusiasm, too often also draw the dollars of local churches as they plan for children, youth, and adult programs. The richer, more formative resources that can help move people's Christian formation and discipleship into periods of growth and maturity are frequently overlooked for a variety of reasons. In either case simply buying, borrowing, or downloading resources keeps the focus on buying the fish someone else has caught and thinks will feed the family well.

Learning to Fish

I learned to fish from my father. He loved fishing small farm ponds as well as modest lakes where he could use a rowboat if he wanted. I think he liked the option of fishing from shore or from out on the water.

I learned first with a bamboo pole that wasn't much longer than I was tall. Swivel, hook on a leader, worm and bobber. Swing the line straight out forward, then back, then forward again, not over the head, not side-arm, just simply forward and back until the line, when dropped, rested as far out as its length permitted. He helped me hook my first bluegill, showed me how to set the hook, pull the fish in rather than yank it out of the water, take the hook out, gently put the little thing back in the water or — joy of joy — put it in the live net because it was actually big enough to keep. I graduated to a closed-face spinning reel on a rod that still wasn't much longer than I was tall. He taught me to cast in our front yard using a dummy plug. There were lots of jerky starts but every once in a while the line sailed out like it was meant to. Aiming was something else. My father bought mini hula hoops and tossed them across the yard as targets. He showed me how to use my wrist to control where the line went. When we went fishing I used my new skills to cast farther and a little more accurately, and to reel in the fish I hooked.

When my hands were big enough and my arms and wrists strong enough and I was tall enough, he brought home a full-sized casting rod, put my spinning reel on it, and returned to the front yard with me. I discovered that the principles of casting were the same but the longer rod required adaptations. It took more "oomph" to get the dummy plug and hence the bobber and hook past the rod's end. It took an adjustment in wrist action to aim straight and true. But the rod also delivered an incredible accuracy as I gradually mastered the finesse of my father's casting. Then, at about age twelve, he introduced me to artificial lures and I was hooked on bass fishing for life. My family would eat the fish we caught. Deep into the Ohio winters we'd have fish rolled in cornmeal and flour and fried in the cast iron skillet.

Last year I picked up a rod and reel for the first time in ages. Everything came back to me — the wrist action, the well aimed cast, the quick toss under overhanging branches, the long low whir as the line spun out across open water, the "Oh crud!" of a cast's miscalculated plunk into the water almost at my feet.

I've come to recognize that somewhere along the way, without really thinking about it, I became able to feed myself if I had to, so long as I could fish.

This chapter is, in a figurative way, about learning to fish relative to Christian faith formation in your setting. As stated above, simply buying, borrowing, or downloading resources for educational and faith formational ministries keeps the focus on buying the fish someone else has caught, processed, packaged, and promoted, and that someone else thinks will feed your faith family well. What I'm going to introduce to you is a process for identifying the content, context, and foundation of educational/faith formational ministry in a local church setting; clarifying the philosophy of educational ministry out of which you work, the theology of educational ministry out of which you work, and the paradigm of educational ministry out of which you work and lead. Yes, I do mean work *and* lead, and will gently tease those two apart later in the chapter. I will, by way of this process, be suggesting the practicality of articulating your own philosophy and theology of Christian education/faith formation and the paradigm of educational ministry out of which you work and lead and even play. Your philosophy, theology, and paradigm of Christian education /faith formation, plus what you identify as content, context, and foundations of educational/faith formational ministry in your particular setting, will then serve as a plumb line for the development of ministries and the selection or creation of appropriate curricular resources.

Often we're tempted to rebel at the prospect of moving through a process. But we need to reconsider. We need to work the process. Working the process will take us from the position of being handed a fish (i.e., a program, a curriculum resource, a bright and shiny product that may well fall short of our expectations) to being able to fish. We can learn to fish in a way that will equip us to feed ourselves and our congregations, not just for a day, a week, a month, or a year, but for a lifetime. We need to learn to fish in a way that is completely portable and adaptable, so that no matter what the environment in which we find ourselves, we can help create and sustain a Christian formational community of faith. We need to learn to fish so if we do go to the market we aren't duped by the hawkers' sales pitches and our own naiveté. We need to learn to fish so that even if we don't necessarily like to do it and would rather pay somebody else to do it, we will nonetheless do it well so that our faith communities do not suffer. We need to learn to fish so we can bring others into the practice of fishing — the practice of faith formational ministries — right alongside us.

Learning to fish relative to Christian faith formation has several phases or "lessons," just like my father's fishing lessons. No, I'm not going to use my childhood narrative as an allegory. You can all breathe a sigh of relief. But since it is the metaphor of choice for this chapter, I'm using it as a framework.

A Word about the Order of the "Lessons"
I'm presenting the process as a series of hands-on lessons in the following order:

Lesson #1: Determining what hours you have available to dedicated to faith formation/educational ministry, and what the emphasis of those hours will be.

Lesson #2: Identifying the core ministry content, that is the driving beliefs and values, of your faith formation/educational ministry.

Lesson #3: Identifying the context of your ministry of faith formation/educational ministry.

Lesson #4: Identifying the foundation statements of your ministry of faith formation/educational ministry.

Lesson #5: Answering the question, what is the philosophy of educational ministry out of which you work?

Lesson #6: Answering the question, what is the theology of educational ministry out of which you work?

Lesson #7: Answering the question, what is the paradigm of educational ministry out of which you work and lead?

If diagrammed, the process would be well suited to a quasi-cyclical model. You could work through the lessons in the order provided and by the end of the process have at least fundamentals. More likely, though, you will have skills and self-confidence to really make a difference for faith formational ministries. Or if you are particularly comfortable thinking and writing in terms of philosophy, theology, and paradigms, you could begin with Lessons #5, 6, and 7, then move to Lessons #1, 2, 3 and 4. Either way will get you there — to be able to help create and sustain a Christian formational community of faith and bring others into the practice of faith formational ministries right alongside you — so long as you don't try short-cuts. Short-cut the process and you short-change yourself and those you serve. Vital congregations don't settle for short-changing their communities of faith.

Lesson #1: "If you could devote only x hours a week to faith formation/ educational ministry...."
In J. Bradley Wigger's *The Power of God at Home*, the author makes the case for families to imbue their daily lives with faith formation.[1] He then points out creative ways this can happen even within the family's crunched time. While working my way though Wigger's book and, by the way, marking it up profusely with underlining and notes in the margin so I could find all

the "good stuff" again (except that it was all good stuff!), I got to musing about what a new model for part-time Christian educators might look like if I adapted Wigger's strategy. Part-time Christian educators' chronic and legitimate lament is that there's always more work to do than paid hours in which to do what's needed in the ten, fifteen, or twenty hours a week of their contract. The educators' recurring solution to this dilemma is to work more hours than they are paid. I sketched out an alternate model I thought might work. When I went back over it in preparation for a workshop at which I would share it for the first time, I realized the model wasn't just for part-time Christian educators. After all, when was the last time a full time Director of Christian Education, Youth Minister, Family Life Minister, Solo, Associate, or Senior Minister in a local church didn't lament having more work — more ministry — than hours in the week to accomplish it? Just about everyone is crunched for time. The key question of my alternate model is equally pivotal for all those involved in the ministries of faith formation and Christian education, full time, part-time, ordained or lay. "If you could devote only x hours per week to faith formation/educational ministry, what's the emphasis that's needed?"

Notice the wording of the question? If you could devote *only* however many hours per week, what's the really critical, absolutely essential, "would make sure it happened even if nothing else did" emphasis? The "could only" qualifier is there on purpose. It forces you and me to review our ministries from a closed quantitative perspective of distinctly limited hours, in order to discern the qualitative perspective of what emphasis is most needed. That insight will then assist us in focusing our ministries and re-ordering our use of those precious yet limited hours.

Point-in-Time Exercise: What's Your "X"?

▓ Begin by determining the value of x for you. For instance, if you are a part-time Christian educator, use the actual number of hours for which you are contracted. If you are a full-time Christian educator, use a 40–50 hour work week. Subtract the number of hours per week that you are fulfilling roles and functions in the local and wider church that are not directly related to your work in faith formation. I know, in Chapters One and Two I pushed hard to expand your concept of what fits into faith formation and Christian education. I'm not about to contradict myself here. However, I know from pastoral experience that myriad hours get allotted to myriad details, plans, programs, and meetings. Not all those hours are spent in intentional, focused ministry. Subtract those hours from the original 40 to find the amount of your x. If you are a local church pastor, full or part-time, ordained or lay, add up the hours you actually have available for intentional faith formation each week. That's your x. Figuratively set that number aside for now. We'll come back to it in a little while.

I imagine that by this point in Lesson #1, some of you are already engaged in what I'll call program triage. By that I mean you're mentally running through the list of faith formation/educational ministry programs and trying to determine which one or two you'd absolutely keep working on, which several you'd have to pass along to someone else if someone else could be found to handle it, and which might get lost altogether. Slow down, though, and take a breath. Put aside the triage chart. I have something very different in mind for us to consider together in answer to the question "If you could devote only x hours per week to faith formation/educational ministry what's the emphasis that's needed?"

I suggest the emphasis be on:

a. Faith formation core ministry content, before curricular resource materials
b. Context and foundation statements, then specifics like program plans and resources
c. Philosophy, theology, and paradigm of educational ministry out of which you work and lead and even play, especially if there's only enough time to do these three elements (philosophy, theology, and paradigm) of educational ministry.

Lesson #2: What's your faith formation/educational ministry core ministry content?
I asked my resident expert on church development, transformational ministry, mission and vision statements, otherwise known as my husband, David, what he'd equate to my term "core ministry content." He answered that it sounded like what many church development people might call primary beliefs and values. I decided to stick with my term, even if it's a little awkward, because I want you to think about faith formation and your orientation to and role in it from outside the more familiar church development box.

An example from my own experience will help illustrate what I mean by core ministry content. As the associate minister of a large suburban church, one of my responsibilities was children's ministry from birth through sixth grade. In retrospect I can clearly see and articulate the content of my ministry with the children and their parents within the community of the congregation. It was advocacy for the children of the church. The advocacy took various forms. One was the conviction that the children were as valuable, essential, worthy of respect, wanted, gifted, vulnerable, and insightful as the adults. Two other forms followed: best practices and best policies.

Best practices meant that the Christian Education Board and I took a long hard look at the long-standing practice of recruiting church school teachers to teach for one quarter at a time. Each class had three different sets of adults working with them over the course of a September-through-May program year. The teaching sets were with their respective classes for about twelve weeks at a time. The system was easy on the adults' schedule, and therefore easier on the Church School Superintendent who had to recruit. However, it was not so good for the children. Just about the time some consistency developed between teacher and class, the teacher left and a new one arrived. We bit the bullet, so to speak, made the dramatic change of recruiting teachers for a full program year rather than quarters, and watched an equally dramatic positive change in children's excitement and engagement levels, attendance, and sense of belonging.

Best practices also meant integrating the children into the "adult" worship service in authentic ways in contrast to gimmicky, aren't-they-cute patronizing and entertainment ways. It meant holding firm about no children's pageant on Christmas Eve because, as our children's choir director so succinctly put it, "No child should ever have to be throwing up on Christmas Eve because they're afraid they'll forget their lines." It meant no playing to the adults during Words with Children in order to get laughs. The pastors, including me at first, found this one particularly challenging. Best practices meant multiple conversations and adjustments of practice regarding children and communion.

Best policies meant, in the bygone days before anyone was creating Safe Church policies, always having to have a signed consent form from the parent or guardian for off-site outings, even if it was a simple walk around the neighborhood to collect canned goods. Best policies meant removing the children's names from any pictures in the church hallways, especially those nearest the nursery and toddler room, to minimize the chance a stranger could take a little one simply by naming her correctly. Unlike the church school teachers, helpers in the nursery were still recruited by the week or month. Then the Nursery Room policy changed so that a year-round attendant was present as well as the weekly volunteers and additional safety procedures were put in place. Safe Church training and the development of comprehensive Safe Church policies were just coming to the foreground and we were gearing up to work through them as I concluded my ministry at that church.

Core ministry content can be as diverse as the persons engaging in it. Mine was advocacy for children within the community of the congregation at one particular setting. In another setting it was the intersection of faith and adult life transitions. Some of my colleagues have named cultivating and sustaining a spiritual home for children, providing for youth to have voice, and creating real help for the real world for parents and children as their diverse core ministry content. They identify fashioning environments of questioning, doubting, dialogue and debate, or engendering faith-informed and faith driven social action and mission as core ministry content. What I want you to notice in this discussion is that not one program gets listed here. I am suggesting that you identify what is at the core of faith formation ministry for you. What is it that frames and propels what you are about when it comes to faith formation?

Point-in-Time Exercise: Frames and Propellants of Your Faith Formation Ministry

- On a piece of paper or its twenty-first century equivalent (e.g., computer, Blackberry, cell phone with all the bells and whistles) complete the following statement:

   My ministry of faith formation will include . . .

- Each time you write down a program or a curricular resource, draw a line through it. Don't erase it. Leave it where you can see it so you know you brought it to mind. There is a clue in the crossed-out item. But draw a line through it and complete the statement again.

- Continue completing the statement, crossing out anything that's actually a program or curricular resource, until you reach the core concept underlying and informing your faith formation orientation. Once you think you have it identified, verify it by cross-checking it against what you actually do in your ministry. Do your actions support what you identified as the core concept? If not, keep working the process until the two align.

   We put a sample of what a list might look like on www.thepilgrimpress.com.

■ Look back over your list. Jot down your reactions to the following:

- What did you discover about your beliefs and values relative to faith formation in the process of completing the exercise?
- What do you know again about yourself and your orientation to faith formation that you may have forgotten or misplaced?
- What do you understand about your faith formation core ministry content that you hadn't realized before?

■ In the example from the ministry experience I shared earlier, advocacy for the children of that faith community was my core ministry content. I could put it into a statement like this: "Advocacy for children frames and propels what I'm about when it comes to faith formation." I invite you to fill in the following statement as a way to articulate your faith formation core ministry content.

_____ frames and propels what I'm about when it comes to faith formation.

■ You will need your list and the statement articulating your faith formation core ministry content later, so please keep them handy.

Lesson #3: What is the Context of Your Ministry of Faith Formation/ Educational Ministry?

In what context are you engaged in ministry? In what context are you actualizing or will you actualize faith formative ministries? Descriptions of contexts may begin with basic demographics — urban, suburban, rural; large, middle-size, small membership; German immigrant founders, predominantly African-American membership, New England Pilgrim roots, Asian-Pacific congregation, multicultural, multi-ethnic, multinational worshippers, congregants of differing sexual orientations; lots of young families, only senior citizens, singles of all ages, college-age influx, aging congregation dwindling in numbers or new influx of members; wealthy professionals, middle class professionals and blue collar workers, working poor, a mix of socio-economic status. That's really just the surface of context, though. Other important descriptors that need naming may include families "pulled three ways from Sunday," poor church school attendance, booming church school attendance, a membership that is happier to lay blame than venture forward. Anyone who's read through a local church profile recognizes which types of information listed above typically is provided, and which isn't. Ethnographic researchers will tell you that the most insight-provocative contextual descriptions are those that are, to use Clifford Geertz's designation, "thick."[2]

Point-in-Time Exercise: A Glimpse at Your Thick Context

■ So, what is the context in which you engage in Christian faith formation? You could spend hours creating a thorough description, and you are of course welcome to do that. In fact, if a group works on this exercise, one strategy for completing it would be to divide it into sections, have everyone take a section to complete in 20–30 minutes, compile the information generated, and finish up by filling in any holes. If you're working up the description yourself and aren't allured by the thought of spending hours on it, stick to what you can compile in 40–45 minutes. I sometimes find it helpful to tackle tasks like this in small chunks, jotting down what comes to mind easily, keeping it close at hand and jotting down more as I think of it. Other times I do the initial jotting, lay the task aside for a while (a couple of hours, a day, a week, when I next clear off my desk), then finish it up. It's not like a test that has a time limit, after all.

We put a worksheet on www.thepilgrimpress.com for your use. It's not meant to be an exhaustive list of the elements of your context, so add others and adapt any as needed.

■ Earlier, in Chapter Two's section on Context and Texts of Faith Formation, you read, "The whole life of the congregation, indeed the life of the church as the body of Christ, is the context and the 'texts' of faith formation. We clergy are good at exegeting biblical texts. What we need to practice is exegeting the life of the local congregation and fashioning ministry from and to it." Looking back over your descriptions as a whole, identify the three that most seem to be driving the congregation currently. Then read over the descriptions again. Identify the three that seem to be driving your ministry currently.

■ Consider each list thoughtfully. If there are discrepancies between them, take a moment and consider why that is, and what it means for your involvement in intentional faith formation in this setting. Do you follow pastoring habits that lock up time and energies which could otherwise be channeled into faith formation practices, study, and involvement? Are you operating within your comfort zone only? What might be required outside of that comfortable area in order for authentic faith formation to be fertilized and nurtured?

If you do some thoughtful exegeting here, what does this context and its "texts" have to say that you need to hear? That the congregation needs to hear? What transcendent Word reveals itself? What movement of the Spirit brushes your soul's cheek and whispers on behalf of the living Body of Christ?

■ Taking into account what you have been exploring and the insights from your exegeting, write in a sentence or two the context for faith formational ministry in which you would be involved in faith formation currently. If you find it helpful, use the following as one way to articulate your context for faith formation ministry.

The context for faith formational ministry in which I would be involved is one in which . . .
The Spirit of God may be speaking within this context . . .

■ You will need your notes from this section, especially your identified context for faith formational ministry, a little later. Please keep them handy.

Now, on to foundation statements.

Lesson #4: What are the Foundation Statements of Your Faith Formation/ Educational Ministry?

I love foundation statements. They are the big, plump, juicy declarations that we can sink our teeth into over and over again and that remind us, each time, of who we are, Whose we are, and by what in God's magnificent name we are determined to be about. Here are six that guide my ministry within and on behalf of the local and wider church particularly with regards to Christian education and faith formation. There are additional foundation statements that guide my ministries in other arenas, but those are for another conversation. I'll stick with these six for our purposes together.

- No one's safety will be compromised.
- Meeting needs, not numbers, is first priority.

- More is not necessarily better; sometimes it's just more.
- Everything I (we) do is educating and forming faith in some way, good or bad. Increase the good; work to decrease and maybe even eliminate the bad.
- My work is a microcosm of the whole, not a piece of it.
- There is enough God, time, energy for what is needed. *There is enough God, time, energy for what is needed.*

If any of these foundation statements resonate with you, feel free to adopt them for yourself. I have come by them organically, having grown up professionally in fields rich in the wisdom, insight, and practice of phenomenal educators and scholars, some of whom predated me and others who have lived concurrent with me. What I articulate as essential foundations for faith formation ministries are deeply rooted in all I have learned, synthesized, taught, reflected on, been challenged by, revised, and been called to live into. In that sense they are original to me, but probably only in that sense.

What are the foundations that undergird faith formative ministries for you? What are the structures that buttress you as you seek to fulfill ministries of authentic faith formation? What are the scaffolds upon which you will actualize faith formative ministries now and in the future? Or, to return to the original metaphor, what are the big, plump, juicy declarations that you and your congregation with you can sink your teeth into over and over again and that remind you, each time, of whom you are, Whose you are, and by what in God's magnificent name you are determined to be about?

I invite you to articulate foundation statements that guide — or could guide, starting now — your ministry within and on behalf of at least the local church particularly with regard to Christian education and faith formation. If you find it helpful, use the sentence stem below.

For me, the following are foundational to faith formational ministry . . .

What WAS the Question?

The question that began all the work you've recently put yourself through — I was going to say it was the work I put you through, but I have no power over that whatsoever, so if you did the work in the sections above, you have only yourself to thank — the question was:

"If you could devote only *x* hours per week to faith formation/educational ministry what's the emphasis that's needed?"

You almost have what you need to answer the question for yourself. You've completed the first four faith formation/educational ministry fishing lessons. Here come the next three in rapid succession.

Lesson #5: What is the Philosophy of Educational Ministry Out of Which You Work?

I can just hear you now. "ARGHHHH — you're making me do a paper!" Nope, not at all. In twenty-five words or more (yes, or more if you wish) write out a coherent statement of your philosophy of educational ministry. I've included the prompts used in the Application for Church Educator Certification of the United Church of Christ as stimulus for your thoughts.[3] Have fun!

- To you, what is the overall purpose of educational ministry?
- What ideas about the ways people learn are reflected in your understanding of educational ministry? You might include:
  - references to teaching styles and learning styles
  - thoughts about resource selection
  - insights into the relationship between church education and other aspects of church life and witness

When you've finished you might want to read it to someone and find out if she or he understands what it is you are stating. I have several friends who do this for me. No matter how clear I try to be, my writing may be as clear as mud to another. The friends, and occasionally students when asked, let me know if the waters are murky or clear, and usually have excellent suggestions for murk-and-mud control.

Lesson #6: What is the Theology of Educational Ministry Out of Which You Work?

Follow the same procedure you used for the philosophy of educational ministry, only this time focus on the theological. Once again I've included the prompts used in the Application for Church Educator Certification of the United Church of Christ as stimulus for your thoughts.[4] Once again, have fun! (I hear that groaning!)

- How is your theology reflected in your understanding of educational ministry? You might include:
  - ways you ground your understanding in scripture
  - insights on the way you view God

- your sense of the role Jesus played/plays in the life of those who follow him
- your perceptions of the work of the Holy Spirit.

Lesson #7: What is the Paradigm of Educational Ministry
Out of Which You Work and Lead and even Play?
According to the *Encarta Dictionary* (English, North America), the noun "paradigm" has four definitions, three of which are helpful to this lesson.[5]

1. Typical example: typical example of something
2. Model that forms basis of something: an example that serves as a pattern or model for something, especially one that forms the basis of a methodology or theory
3. Relationship of ideas to one another: in the philosophy of science, a generally accepted model of how ideas relate to one another, forming a conceptual framework within which scientific research is carried out.

I have several paradigms out of which I work when it comes to educational ministry. One is process — no surprise there, I suspect. The chapters of this book are filled with process: providing you, the reader, processes to use in your ministry; constructing processes with you in mind and then leading you through them. I approach the college courses I teach, the committee work I'm part of at the local church or the campus, and just about everything else that's explicitly or implicitly linked with ministry and education from the paradigm of process. In fact, this past year my specific role on one task force was to address and integrate into our work elements and strategies of process.

Co-learner is a second paradigm out of which I work and lead relative to educational ministry. Number three, a sibling of my second paradigm, is teacher and mentor of future colleagues/professional peers. This third one is particularly relevant in the college professor/college student setting, but also helps inform the work I'm privileged to have in partnership with novice church educators and clergy.

These paradigms function as parts of a whole for me. Stated in terms of the definitions of paradigm above, they are a few of the models that form the basis of both theory and methodology relative to Christian faith formation. Taken together they help create a relationship of ideas to one another, thus forming a conceptual framework within which Christian faith formational ministry is carried out.

Okay, it's your turn. What is the paradigm of educational ministry out of which you work and lead and even play? Have fun! This is what you already know even if you don't yet know that you know it! Here's a sentence stem that may be helpful.

One paradigm of educational/faith formational ministry out of which I work and lead and even play is . . .

Put this statement where you can see it.

Put It Together and What Do You Get?

Visually pull the notes from your Fishing Lessons together. What's the number of hours you calculated in this chapter's first Point-in-Time Exercise? Put your educational philosophy, theology of Christian educational ministry, and paradigm(s) out of which you work and lead and play relative to educational/faith formational ministry next to each other. Next to them, or right below them, put the summary statements about core ministry content, context, and foundation statements. You may need to use a dining room or fellowship hall table!

Taken together, determine what *emphasis* needs those limited but dedicated hours the most. If you list a specific program, "Go directly to jail," as it says in the Monopoly board game, "do not pass GO, do not collect $200." Name the emphasis, not the how of the emphasis just yet. Remember what I stated earlier in the chapter about working the process, learning to fish, becoming the one who can bring others of the congregation into the practice of fishing — selecting, creating, and sustaining faith formational ministries — right alongside you. That said, even if you did have to go to metaphorical jail for a turn, it's now time to put a clear statement together.

"If I could only devote _____ hours per week to faith formation/educational ministry, the emphasis that's needed is . . ."

Reordering the Hours: A New Model for Those Responsible for Faith Formation/Educational Ministry

My mother, now deceased, decided to go to counseling about a year after my father's death. She was quite faithful in her appointments. Frequently she spoke with me about the things she talked about in the sessions and the questions the counselor posed. She was more content than she had been for a long time. Then suddenly she stopped going. When she told me she wasn't going back, that she didn't see the need for it any more, I asked her why. From her answers it was clear she was disgusted by the turn the focus of the sessions had taken. I was finally able to piece together that so long as Mom was getting to talk about her life, her circumstances, her past, her reactions to my father's death, and so on, getting counseling was a positive experience. The minute the counselor turned the focus to changes she would have to make in her own behaviors in order to move forward in her life, she'd had enough.

Those who would be faithful in Christian formation/educational ministries need to spend those precious limited hours per week in ways that move us and our congregations forward. That means we need to be willing to reorder our use of those hours based on the emphasis that, we've learned, most needs our attention. Otherwise all we've done is told ourselves our own story and then walked away, disgusted that changes in behavior must come next.

Those who would take on the mantle of Christian educator/faith former must both work at educational ministries and faith formation *and* lead. It doesn't matter if you are ordained, commissioned, or licensed ministers or professional or lay church educators, you must invest your time in discerning and leading, preparing to lead, learning ever more then leading and pointing the way. If the Christian educator/faith former is not out in front, educational ministry and faith formation will meander at best, become rote, or even stagnate to a living death. Christian educators already understand that this can't be done by merely perusing and ordering from resource catalogues, recruiting warm bodies, and showing up on Sunday morning.

Educators/faith formers are the visionaries who know how to implement the concrete, and also how to discern and identify others for the educational/ faith formational ministry of that local church. They are the ones who know how to equip others for ministries within that particular setting. They lead by more than example alone. They lead by advocacy and modeling. They also lead by transparent transformation. When they themselves are transformed because of what they themselves are doing, it is so transparent that others catch fire or are willing to take a risk along with them. They can go places, and take the congregation where they had no clue they were going before, and ministry together is blessed.

If you count yourself among those just mentioned — and indeed I hope you do or soon will — take up the challenge of creating a new model and practice for engaging in educational/faith formational ministries by reordering those hours, few or many as they may be. Be clear about the theological and biblical plumb line for deciding what gets the most attention and what will not and why. Don't just keep doing the same-old, same-old. Rigorously examine everything in light of your emphasis statement. Yes, that includes confirmation! Make adjustments. Review resources through the perspectives you've gained. Returning to the fishing metaphor . . . exercise those fishing sensibilities!

If there is no trained Christian educator in your congregation and you yourself aren't especially well trained in educational ministries either, create ways to correct that. Borrow books from libraries and colleagues. Start attending workshops offered in your area. Read the denominational web pages and the web pages of professional Christian education organizations such as the Association of United Church Educators. Create your own learning group within the congregation. Use the process in this chapter to help focus your singular or group efforts and to discern the resources that foster your fishing skills. Most of all get in there, learn to fish and enjoy the feast!

Six

Commission, Not Conclusion: Picking Up the Mantle of Faith Formation for Vital Congregations

While reading N.T. Wright's *The Last Word: Scripture and the Authority of God — Getting Beyond the Bible Wars*, **I came across his description of improvisation:**

The notion of "improvising" is important, but sometimes misunderstood. As all musicians know, improvisation does not at all mean a free-for-all where "anything goes," but precisely a disciplined and careful listening to all the other voices around us, and a constant attention to the themes, rhythms and harmonies of the complete performance so far, the performance which we are now called to continue. At the same time, of course, it invites us, while being fully obedient to the music so far, and fully attentive to the voices around us, to explore fresh expressions, provided they will eventually lead to that ultimate resolution.[1]

Wright was suggesting the role of improvisation in the study, discussion, understanding, and interpretation of New Testament scriptures. I find his description of improvisation to be a compelling framework or mode of operation for credible educational and faith formative ministry in the church no matter the church's size, shape, or context, and so have reworked Wright's description to that end:

> As all those engaged in it know, Christian education/faith formation does not at all mean a free-for-all where "anything goes," but precisely a disciplined and careful listening to all the other voices around us, and a constant attention to the themes, rhythms and harmonies of the complete ministries so far, the ministries which we are now called to continue. At the same time, of course, it invites us, while being fully obedient to the educational/faith formational ministry so far, and fully attentive to the voices around us, to explore fresh expressions, provided they will eventually lead to that ultimate resolution into "faith formation [as] our participation in God's work of inviting persons into relationship with God, self, others, and creation. . . . [while] the faith community's role in this process is to participate in God's work by creating an intentional process of developing identity and vocation within [the Christian] tradition."[2]

Throughout this book I've attempted to lead you into closer contact with "a disciplined and careful listening to all the other voices around us" so that authentic, meaningful, transformational faith formational/educational ministries might be discerned, fashioned, piloted, assessed, adjusted, and celebrated. You've read over and over again my conviction that Christian education, educational ministry, faith formation . . . all of it is interrelated. By now I'm sure you have also recognized that Christian education, educational ministry, faith formation . . . none of it is for wimps.

Vital congregations are congregations and congregational leaders who, despite the challenges, seek the ways and means of cultivating environments conducive to and supportive of faith formative ministries for all within the congregation and even those beyond the congregation itself. Vital congregations find or make ways for the ministries of faith formation to be *vigorous*, even when those ministries are low-key and subtle. Just how each of us and our congregations does this will take a good-size dose of improvisation —

something local churches may or may not be terribly comfortable doing at first. But please don't let that inhibit or stop you. May what you've discovered within these pages, within yourself, and within the congregation you serve be just the beginning of your vital ministry of faith formation among the current and yet-to-be members of the living Body of Christ. Blessings to each of you.

Notes

Introduction

1 The good work done by Dorothy Bass and her colleagues in the Valparaiso Project on practices of faith is reawakening an interest in and appreciation for the relevance of ancient practices for Christian living and spiritual wholeness in our lives of faith and faithfulness in the complex, often overwhelming, anxious twenty-first century. Equally important is the work of Richard Foster, Joyce Rupp, Thomas Moore, Joan Chittister and others in resurrecting foundational Christian spiritual disciplines, many of which were dropped by the wayside as churches and denominations were challenged by seismic shifts in culture — first by the Industrial Revolution, then by the technology explosion, and then by all the ramifications of the modern and post-modern ages. Page through denominational book and resource catalogues or go to the online websites and you will find fine materials to assist individuals and church leaders in understanding and adopting these disciplines into their lives.

2 In a different but no less important vein is the work of leaders such as Bill Esaum and Tom Bandy, Walt Kallestad, and Paul Nixon on transforming local churches to mission-ing and disciple-ing communities of faith.

3 In still another vein comes ongoing work with Howard Gardner's theory of multiple intelligences and the adult learner that continues to enrich our understanding of the role intelligences such as kinesthetic, musical, interpersonal and intrapersonal have in connecting people with the living heritage of the Christian faith, fruitful discipleship, and engagement with the biblical texts. We are coming to realize that the cognitive (i.e., the verbal + written + logical) approaches such as we see in traditional sermons, lectures, and start-here-and-go-to-there teaching styles are not enough to provide satisfying Christian formation experiences. Tapping the full collection of multiple intelligences enhances individuals' ability to engage in and deepen their Christian life of faith and discipleship.

Chapter One

1 From Rev. Dr. Marian R. Plant, "Christian Education: For Just Such a Time as This" (sermon, First Congregational (United Church of Christ), Lockport, IL, September 26, 1999).

2 In his book *Christian Religious Education: Sharing Our Story and Vision* (Harper & Row: San Francisco 1980), p. 7, Thomas Groome discusses the limitations of passing on what is "already known" through a model Paulo Friere describes as a "banking concept of education" in *Pedagogy of the Oppressed*, trans.,

Myra Berger Ramos (Seabury Press: New York, 1970), pp. 58ff.

3 From Marian R. Plant, "The Development of Faith Maturity in Men and Implications for Education in the Local Church" (PhD diss., College of Education, Northern Illinois University, 1998), p. 142.

4 Ibid., p. 151.

5 See descriptions regarding assessment principles and best educational practices provided by Karen B. Tye in her book *Basics of Christian Education* (Chalice Press: St. Louis, MO 2000), and by Elliot W. Eisner in his book *The Educational Imagination: On the Design and Evaluation of School Programs* (Merrill Prentice Hall: Columbus, OH 3rd ed. 2002).

6 John Dewey, *Experience and Education* (1938; repr., Collier Books: New York 1975), p. 25.

7 Jim Wilhoit, *Christian Education and the Search for Meaning* (Baker Book House: Grand Rapids, MI 2nd ed. 1991), pp. 9–10.

8 Sondra Higgins Matthaei, "Rethinking Faith Formation" in *Religious Education* (Winter 2004): p. 57, referring to Matthei, Making Disciples: Faith Formation in the Wesleyan Tradition (Abingdon Press: Nashville, TN 2000), p. 22.

9 Ibid.

10 Ibid.

11 Ibid.

Chapter Two

1 Howard P. Colson and Raymond M. Rigdon, *Understanding Your Church's Curriculum* , rev. ed. (Broadman Press: Nashville, TN 1981), p. 40.

2 Maria Harris, *Fashion Me a People: Curriculum in the Church* (Westminster John Knox Press: Louisville, KY 1989), p. 63.

3 Ibid., p. 17.

4 Ibid.

5 Ibid.

6 Staci Williams, student course assignment (Defiance College, Defiance, OH, 2006).

7 Mary Winters, student course assignment (Defiance College, Defiance, OH, 2006).

8 Thomas H. Groome, *Christian Religious Education: Sharing Our Story and Vision* (Harper & Row: San Francisco 1980), pp. 15, 25.

9 Roger L. Shinn, "The educational ministry of the church" in Marvin J. Taylor, ed., *An Introduction to Christian Education* (Abingdon Press: Nashville, TN 1966), p. 19.

10 Abigail Richard, student course assignment (Defiance College, Defiance, OH, 2006).

11 Christopher Beck, student course assignment (Defiance College, Defiance, OH, 2006).

12 Mary Winters, student course assignment (Defiance College, Defiance, OH, 2006).

13 See John 11:1–44, especially verse 44.

14 Since the publication of his book *Frames of Mind: The Theory of Multiple Intelligences* (Basic Books: New York 1983), Howard Gardner has identified an eighth intelligence, naturalistic, and has investigated the possibility of at least two others, spiritual intelligence and existential intelligence. See Howard Gardner, *Intelligence Reframed: Multiple Intelligences for the 21st Century* (Basic Books: New York 1999), p. 47.

15 Jerry Larsen, *Religious Education and the Brain: A Practical Resource for Understanding How We Learn about God* (Paulist Press: New York 2000), pp. 124–125.

16 Larsen, pp. 125–130.

17 Ibid., p.125.

18 Ibid., p. 126.

19 Ibid.

20 Ibid., p. 128.

21 Ibid.

22 Ibid.

23 Ibid., p. 130.

24 *Common Miracles — The New American Revolution in Learning*, video cassette, directed by George Paul (MPI Home Video: Oak Forest, IL 1993).

25 *Chariots of Fire*, DVD, directed by Hugh Hudson (Warner Home Video: New York 1986).

26 Gary E. Moore, "Cone of Learning (Edgar Dale)," slide no. 12 in presentation, "What is SAE?," http://www.cals.ncsu.edu/agexed/sae/ppt1/sld012.htm (accessed February 16, 2008). Adapted from Edgar Dale's *Audio-visual Methods in Teaching* (Holt, Rinehart, and Winston: New York 3rd ed. 1969), p. 108.

27 Jerry Larsen, *Religious Education and the Brain: A Practical Resource for Understanding How We Learn about God* (Paulist Press: New York 2000), p. 132.

28 Sondra Higgins Matthaei, "Rethinking Faith Formation" in *Religious Education* (Winter 2004): p. 57, referring to Matthei, *Making Disciples: Faith Formation in the Wesleyan Tradition* (Abingdon: Nashville Press, TN 2000), p. 22.

Chapter Three

1 J. Bradley Wigger, *The Power of God at Home: Nurturing Our Children in Love and Grace* (Jossey-Bass: San Francisco 2003).

2 Dr. Seuss [Theodor S. Geisel], *How the Grinch Stole Christmas* (1957; repr., Random House, Inc.: New York 2007), pp. 5, 50.

3 Ibid., p. 5.

4 J. Bradley Wigger, *The Power of God at Home: Nurturing Our Children in Love and Grace* (Jossey-Bass: San Francisco 2003).

5 Ibid., p. 59.

6 Janet Lurhs, *The Simple Living Guide: A Sourcebook for Less Stressful, More Joyful Living* (Broadway Books: New York, 1997); Michael Schut, ed., *Simpler Living, Compassionate Life: A Christian Perspective* (Living the Good News: Denver 1999).

7 Anne Colby and William Damon, *Some Do Care: Contemporary Lives of Moral Commitment* (Free Press: New York 1992); Laurent A. Parks Daloz, Cheryl H. Keen, James P. Keen, and Sharon Daloz Parks, *Common Fire: Leading Lives of Commitment in a Complex World* (Beacon Press: Boston 1996).

8 Staci Williams, "Christmas Gift Bags" in *Direct Current: Practical Ideas for Local Church Ministries* (Defiance College), 1, no. 1 (Advent 2007): p. 2.

9 Ibid.

Chapter Four

1 Wright, N. T., *The Last Word: Scripture and the Authority of God — Getting Beyond the Bible Wars* (HarperSanFrancisco: San Francisco 2005), p. 96.

2 Ibid.

3 Adapted from discussions during the 2007 Seminar by the Sea Clergy Conference, Myrtle Beach, SC, March 6–10, 2007.

4 N. T. Wright, p. 95 (emphasis added).

5 Dave Ramsey, *Financial Peace Revisited* (Viking Press: New York 2003).

6 Ibid., pp. 90–92. See also Debt Snowball worksheets in Dave Ramsey's *Financial Peace University* (The Lampo Group, Inc.: Brentwood, TN 2006), pp. 116–117.

7 Wright, p. 140.

8 A paraphrase of Dennis Waitley's "Most people overestimate what they can do in a year and underestimate what they can do in five," heard at a workshop led by David G. Plant. The originator of the paraphrase is unknown.

9 Hypothetical example of the author's own creation.

10 Paul J. Achtemeier, ed., *The HarperCollins Bible Dictionary* (HarperSanFrancisco: San Francisco 1996).

11 Barbara J. Essex, *Bible for Vital Congregations* (The Pilgrim Press: Cleveland 2008).

12 *Genesis: A Living Conversation* , video cassette, directed by Catherine Tatge (Films for the Humanities: Princeton, NJ 1996).

13 *From Jesus to Christ. The First Christians* , video cassette, directed by

William Cran (PBS Home Video: Alexandria, VA 1998).

14 *Peter and Paul and the Christian Revolution*, video cassette, directed by Margaret Koval (PBS Home Video: Alexandria, VA 2002).

15 Bryan Sirchio, *Bugs for Lunch*, audio cassette (Crosswind Music: Madison, WI 1991).

16 Bryan Sirchio, *Come As U R*, audio cassette (Crosswind Music: Madison, WI 1991).

17 Sirchio, *Bugs for Lunch*.

18 Tim Rice and Andrew Lloyd Webber, *Jesus Christ Superstar*, sound recording (Decca: New York 1970).

19 Stephen Schwartz, *Godspell*, sound recording (Bell: New York 1972).

20 Adapted from George Rawson, "We Limit Not the Truth of God" as printed in *Pilgrim Hymnal* (The Pilgrim Press: Boston 1966).

Chapter Five

1 J. Bradley Wigger, *The Power of God at Home: Nurturing Our Children in Love and Grace* (Jossey-Bass: San Francisco 2003).

2 Clifford Geertz, "Thick Description: Toward an Interpretive Theory of Culture," in *The Interpretation of Cultures: Selected Essays* (Basic Books: New York 1973), pp. 3–30.

3. From Committee on Certification for Church Educators, United Church of Christ, "Section 5: What Is Church Education? (Your understanding of educational ministry)" in *Application for Certification in Church Education in the United Church of Christ*, p. 14. Available at http://www.ucc.org/education/certified-educators/.

4 Ibid.

5 *MSN Encarta*, s.v. "paradigm," http://encarta.msn.com/dictionary_/paradigm.html, accessed September 15, 2008.

Chapter Six

1 N.T. Wright, *The Last Word: Scripture and the Authority of God — Getting Beyond the Bible Wars* (HarperSanFrancisco: San Francisco 2005), pp. 126–127.

2 Sondra Higgins Matthaei, "Rethinking Faith Formation" in *Religious Education* (Winter 2004): p. 57, referring to Matthei, *Making Disciples: Faith Formation in the Wesleyan Tradition* (Abingdon Press: Nashville, TN 2000), p. 22.

Recommended Resources —
Just to Get You Started

By the time you are reading and using this book there will be new resources for congregational and personal use to assist in the vitalizing of your setting. I hope the ones listed below — certainly not an exhaustive list by any means — whet your appetite and fuel your energies.

Resources for the Restorative Theme of Sabbath

Bass, Dorothy C. *Receiving the Day: Christian Practices for Opening the Gift of Time* . San Francisco: Jossey-Bass Publishers, 2000.

Edwards, Tilden. *Sabbath Time*. Rev. ed. Nashville, TN: Upper Room Books, 2003.

Muller, Wayne. *Sabbath: Finding Rest, Renewal, and Delight in Our Busy Lives*. New York: Bantam Books, 2000.

Ringwald, Christopher D. *A Day Apart: How Jews, christians, and Muslims Find Faith, Freedom, and Joy on the Sabbath*. New York: Oxford University Press, 2007.

Schaper, Donna. *Sabbath Keeping* . Boston: Cowley Publications, 1999.

———. *Sabbath Sense: A Spiritual Antidote for the Overworked*. Minneapolis: Augsburg Books, 2005.

Wigger, J. Bradley. *The Power of God at Home: Nurturing Our Children in Love and Grace*. San Francisco: Jossey-Bass, 2003.

Resources for the Restorative Theme of Abundant Life

Lurhs, Janet. *The Simple Living Guide: A Sourcebook for Less Stressful, More Joyful Living*. New York, Broadway Books, 1997.

Schut, Michael, editor. *Simpler Living, Compassionate Life: A Christian Perspective*. Denver: Living the Good News, 1999.

Resources for the Restorative Theme of the Common Good

Colby, Anne and William Damon. *Some Do Care: Contemporary Lives of Moral Commitment*. New York: Free Press, 1992.

Parks Daloz, Laurent A., Cheryl H. Keen, James P. Keen, and Sharon Daloz Parks. *Common Fire: Leading Lives of Commitment in a Complex World*. Boston: Beacon Press, 1997.

Rosenberger, Dale. *Outreach and Mission for Vital Congregations*. Cleveland: The Pilgrim Press, 2007.

Additional Resources for Re-establishing Homes of Faith and Formation

Beckwith, Ivy. *Postmodern Children's Ministry: Ministry to Children in the 21st Century*. Grand Rapids, MI: Zondervan, 2004.

Caldwell, Elizabeth F. *Making a Home for Faith: Nurturing the Spiritual Life of Your Children*. Cleveland: The Pilgrim Press, 2000.

———. *Leaving Home with Faith: Nurturing the Spiritual Life of Our Youth*. Cleveland: The Pilgrim Press, 2002.

Downing, Sue. *Hand in Hand: Growing Spiritually with Our Children*. Nashville, TN: Discipleship Resources, 1998.

Wehrheim, Carol A. *Getting it Together: Spiritual Practices for Faith, Family, and Work*. Louisville, KY: Westminster John Knox Press, 2002.